# Research Alert Yearbook 2019

Anne C. Whitaker
Editor, Research Alert Newsletter

Whitaker & Company, Publishers, Inc.

# Contents

# Chapter 1

# Alcohol

## Luxury Wines and Spirits Market Seen Growing to $1.122 Trillion by 2022

The global market for luxury wines and spirits was valued at $812.11 billion in 2015, and is expected to reach $1.122 trillion by 2022, supported by a CAGR of 4.8% during 2016 – 2022, according to a new study by Allied Market Research.

The wine segment was a major revenue contributor for global luxury wines and spirits market in 2015. The European region held the leading position in the global market in 2015, and is expected to maintain its lead during the forecast period.

Consumption of luxury wines and spirits has seen a significant growth in the past few years. Further the use of technology has enabled to select the finest quality of raw materials for fermentation to yield quality wines for aging process and consumption.

The wines segment is expected to grow at a faster rate during the forecast period, as the market currently offers alcoholic drinks such as vodka, gin, rum, and brandy and ha s more alcohol by volume (ABV) than other alcoholic beverages. The market has seen a significant growth, owing to increase in popularity of cocktail drinks. Moreover, they ar e being preferred over beers and other alcoholic beverages due to growing popularity o f cognac and tequila. However, there is a decline in the growth of rum and vodka.

SOURCE: *Luxury Wines and Spirits Market,* Allied Market Research, David Correa, 800-792-5285

## Here Are the 10 Brands Bartenders Most Often Recommend

For the second consecutive year, Patron leads the list, followed by:

| Category | Recipient | Recipient | Comments |
|---|---|---|---|
| **Blended Scotch** | Johnnie Walker | Johnnie Walker | Ranked first since the inception of the MORBAs in 2005 |
| **Cognac** | Hennessy | Hennessy | Ranked first for seven of the last |
| **Cordial** | Grand | Grand | Sixth consecutive year with |
| **Coffee Cordial** | Baileys | Baileys | The leader for the six years the category has been included |
| **Flavor Spirits** | BACARDÍ Flavors | Absolut Vodka | Leads for the first time since 2007, overtaking Absolut |
| **Gin** | Bombay | Hendricks | Wins the MORBA for the first |
| **Rum** | BACARDÍ | BACARDÍ | Ranked first for the 12th |
| **Shot/** | Jack | Fireball | First-time lead, displacing |
| **Single Malt** | The Macallan | The Macallan | Its second straight year, having displaced The Glenlivet in 2017 |
| **Tequila** | Patrón | Patrón | Ranked first since 2008 |
| **Vodka** | Grey Goose | Grey Goose | First in all but one year of the study, where it tied with Absolut |
| **Whiskey** | Jack Daniel's | Jack Daniel's | Ranked first for each year the category has been included |

**SOURCE:** MetrixLab MSS Most Often Recommended Brand Award, Kevin Moran, MetrixLab, (+1) 602 698 4053, kevin.moran@us.metrixlab.com

## How Newer Ready-to-Drink Beverages and Packages Are Shaking Up the Adult Beverage Market

Today's consumers are living in a golden era; innovation is everywhere, and choices have never been so abundant. When it comes to brands, there has never been a more challenging time to stay on top of consumers' minds...and in shopping baskets. And looking across consumer packaged goods (CPG) categories, few could be considered as jam-packed with competition as the adult beverage category.

Bad news for most alcohol brands, though, Americans aged 21 and over aren't increasing their alcohol intake the way they're increasing their intake of media. Unless you're thinking "outside the bottle", growth is often fleeting.

**Ready-to-Drink is Tomorrow's Off-Premise Growth Driver**

While price is likely the most well-established purchase driver across the CPG space, convenience often runs a close second. And from a retail perspective, it's an attribute that's boosting sales in categories that previously weren't very convenient.

Ready-to-drink adult beverages means consumers no longer need to visit their favorite bar for that just-perfect cosmopolitian — allowing them the same freedom that beer drinkers have enjoyed for decades. Newer alternative packaging — cans, boxes, etc.—are playing a role as well, as they provide for more convenient and portable options.

That freedom will lead to growing sales in the ready-to-drink cocktail space, which consumers rank highest among the factors driving purchase intent.

**Convenience is King for Ready-to-Drink Cocktails**

*Reasons consumers purchase single-serve ready-to-drink cocktails*

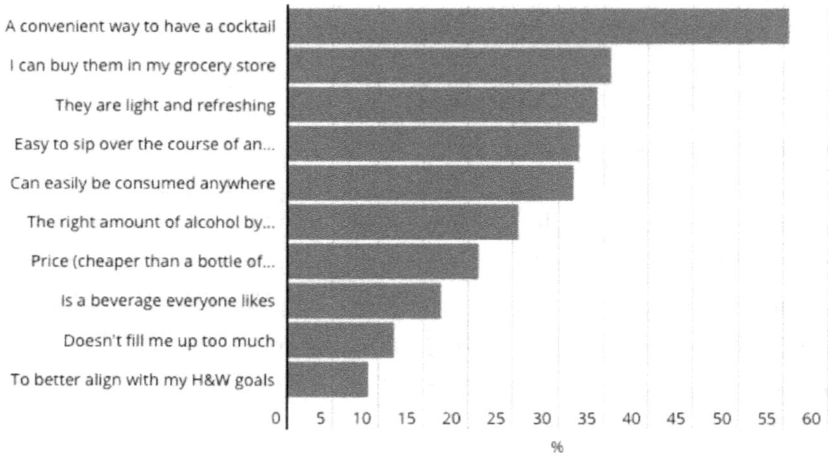


*Credit: Nielsen*

But the ready-to-drink realm isn't only reserved for cocktails. The space is boosting sales across all alcoholic beverage categories, with the emerging malt-based cocktail segment leading the pack in growth. Annual sales in this segment are up 574%, and malt-based cocktails now account for $4.7 million in annual sales.

Commonly available in smaller size packages, spirit- and wine-based "ready to drink cocktails" are also more established and as a result generate larger sales ($62 million and $83 million in annual sales, respectively). And while spirit- and wine-based ready to drink cocktail sales aren't skyrocketing the way malt-based cocktail sales are, they are growing exceptionally well. They both posted sales growth close to 40% higher in the latest 52 weeks compared with sales from a year ago.

**Beyond the Bottle**

It's important to note that the ready-to-drink trend has broadened the scope for how alcoholic beverages have traditionally been contained. Specifically, cans and boxes are steadily growing as popular vessels for ready-to-drink adult beverages, with cans in particular performing well.

When it comes to the craft beer category, cans now account for just over 36% of dollar sales, up 25.4 percentage points since the 52 weeks ended April 25, 2015. In terms of dollar sales, canned craft is now an $820 million sub-category, up from $436 million back in April 2015. But cans are no longer just for beer. There are now 22 wine brands that can 386 different wine items and generate more than $81 million in annual sales. A year ago, canned wine accounted for about $46 million in annual sales.

Single-serve, ready-to-drink cocktails are tapping into an easy way to quench consumers when they're relaxing, unwinding, hitting the beach, cooking outside and many other opportunities when they're away from their favorite bar or restaurant, or outside of their home.

Generationally, younger adults are more likely to gravitate towards ready-to-drink cocktails at social gatherings and outdoor activities. During summer, outdoor picnics, the beach/pool and while traveling/on vacation are popular ready-to-drink occasions among all consumers (32%, 28% and 23%, respectively).

**Top Ready-to-Drink Occasions**

Consumers are looking for convenience, and ready-to-drink cocktails provide consumers with something they've historically had to be at a bar or restaurant to enjoy.

These newer alcohol segments are providing expansion opportunities within the broader alcohol category, manifested in multiple ways:

- New entrepreneurial companies are introducing their brands to the market
- Existing companies are acquiring other brand(s)
- Existing brands in single alcohol segments are extending their name recognition into newer segments to try and become a "power" brand.

Across the board, however, the common bond for success is standing out from the crowd and meeting changing consumer needs.

**SOURCE:** Nielsen, 85 Broad St, New York, NY 10004, (646) 654-5000

## New Consumer Research Shows Strong Interest in Sustainable Wine

There's high interest in purchasing sustainably produced wine in the future, a favorable perception of sustainable certification programs and certification logos, and a willingness to pay more for sustainably produced wine, particularly by Millennials and Gen Z.

That's the conclusion of research by Lulie Halstead, CEO, Wine Intelligence, presented at the first U.S. Sustainable Winegrowing Summit-West.

While organic wine is more universally understood, sustainably produced wine has the highest future purchase consideration, with 74% of U.S. respondents indicating that they would consider buying sustainably produced wine in the future.

In Canada, Sweden and the UK, sustainably produced wine had the highest percentages for future purchase consideration – 70%, 60% and 63% respectively, except in Sweden where organic still ranked higher (68%).

The survey also questioned affinity ("right for me") and sustainably produced again performed well across countries – U.S. (68%), Canada (65%), Sweden (60%) and UK (56%).

For U.S. consumers, sustainable wine is most strongly associated with U.S. States and, in particular, California.

Millennials lead the way in purchasing from the range of sustainably and environmentally produced wine, and nine in 10 are "willing to pay" more for sustainably produced wine. Among all U.S. wine consumers, $3 was the average extra value that consumers indicated they were "willing to pay" for a sustainably produced wine.

Younger consumers (Millennials and Gen Z of legal drinking age) are significantly more engaged with sustainability, viewed as increasingly important to protect the future, and sustainable wine certifications have a strong appeal for younger drinkers, particularly Millennials.

Consumers seek easy ways to find and identify sustainable wine such as clear and simple visual cues or clearly identified sections in a store. Sustainability certifications for wine provide transparency and reassurance. While "Award Winning" endorsements deliver the most reassurance and positive impact on likelihood to buy, both CSWA's Certified California Sustainable Winegrowing (California CERTIFIED SUSTAINABLE) logo and a generic Certified Sustainable logo were viewed as credible and visually appealing. When explicitly tested, wine endorsed with a CSWA logo yields the highest likelihood to buy among U.S. wine consumers.

While winery websites and wine tasting events are more effective at communicating wine sustainability, wine labels and peer recommendation are more frequently used sources.

**Sources:** Wine Intelligence, consumer focus groups in LA, April 2019, n=3 groups; Wine Intelligence, Vinitrac© U.S. (n=2,000), Canada (n=2,479), Sweden (n=1,000) and U.K. (n=1,000), April 2019 U.S., Canadian, Swedish and U.K. regular wine drinkers.

Six states were represented among the 65 summit attendees at the inaugural U.S. Sustainable Winegrowing Summit | West, which included regional winery and vineyard associations, grower and vintner leaders, and other organizations committed to the sustainability of local vineyards, wineries and regions. Several panels explored "the value of sustainability" from the perspective of vineyards and wineries, other industries and trade, as well as lessons learned from various U.S. state sustainability programs. A second Summit, the U.S. Sustainable Winegrowing Summit | East will be held in New York in 2020.

# Chapter 2

# Brands

## The 10 Most Valuable Global Retail Brands in 2019

The most valuable retail brands in the world experienced a 33% growth in brand value this year, according to new data from BrandZ. Reaching a total of $1.4 trillion, the top 75 most valuable brands saw their worth increase by $339 billion from last year.

Brand value is defined as "the dollar amount a brand contributes to the overall value of a corporation." BrandZ arrives at its brand value by multiplying the brand's financial value (the amount of corporate earnings attributed to a particular brand) by brand contribution (a percentage of financial value).

Topping the list as the most valuable retail brand once again is Amazon. They increased their Brand Value by over 91% from 2018, bringing their 2019 value to $315.5 billion. Amazon's Brand Value is more than the next three most valuable brands combined.

Despite Amazon's reputation taking a hit as consumer question its ethics, the ecommerce giant's value to consumers has stayed intact as it has made itself almost indispensable – and the first product search destination for online shoppers.

Second is Alibaba Group, the Chinese conglomerate is considered the world's largest online and mobile commerce business. Their 2019 Brand Value is $131.2 billion, a 48% increase from last year. McDonald's follows closely behind with an increase of 18% from last year, making their Brand Value $130.4 billion.

The Home Depot, the U.S. home improvement giant, ranked 4th on the list with a Brand Value of $53.5 billion.

Taking the 5th spot is Nike, whose Brand Value rose 38% between 2018 and 2019 to $47.4 billion.

The brands rounding out the top 10 are as follows:

- Louis Vuitton (#6 – Brand Value: $47.2 billion)
- Starbucks (#7 – Brand Value: $45.9 billion)
- CHANEL (#8 – Brand Value: $37.0 billion)
- Walmart (#9 – Brand Value: $36.8 billion)
- Hermes (#10 – Brand Value: $31.0 billion)

**SOURCE:** BrandZ, 3 World Trade Center, 175 Greenwich St, 35th Floor, New York, NY 10007

## Consumers Losing Faith in Brands, Say Too Many Use Social Issues as Marketing Ploy

Just one-third of consumers (34%) trust the majority of brands they use or buy, this according to a 2019 Edelman Trust Barometer Special Report, *In Brands We Trust?*. Edelman surveyed 16,000 in eight countries who said that brand trust (81%) was a deciding factor or deal breaker when deciding on a purchase, only quality (85%), convenience (84%), value (84%) and ingredients (82%) were higher.

For the majority of consumers across geographies, age groups, gender and income levels, trust is a big consideration when purchasing. Among reasons for why trust is increasingly becoming more important to consumers is because of their growing concerns about product experience (62%), along with the fast pace of innovation and their increasing reliance on brands for automation; customer experience (55%), including brands' collecting consumers' personal data and tracking and targeting them; and brands' impact on society (69%), including consumers' expectation that brands will help express their values.

"Trust has always played an important role in brand purchase," said Richard Edelman, president and CEO of Edelman. "But consumers now have much larger expectations of brands, and their trust is predicated on how well a brand can pass through the three gates of trust—product, customer experience and impact on society."

Consumers will reward brands that build trust. A majority of consumers who trust a brand are more than twice as likely to be the first to buy the brand's new product (53% versus 25%). They are also more than twice as likely to stay loyal to a brand they trust, even when trendy or innovative competitors come along (62% versus 29%).

Just over half of consumers are twice as likely to support brands they trust (51% versus 24%), and nearly twice as likely to defend it when things go wrong (43% versus 22%). Furthermore, when a brand is trusted on product, customer service and societal impact, the percentage of consumers who will buy first, stay loyal to, advocate for and defend it (68%) is 21 points higher than consumers who buy on product trust only (47%).

However, brands are currently failing the trust test — despite its importance. Most respondents believe every brand has a responsibility to get involved in at least one social issue that does not directly impact its business (53%), yet less than one-fourth (21%) claim to know from personal experience that the brands they use keep the best interests of society in mind.

More than half of respondents (56%) said that too many brands are using societal issues as a marketing ploy. And consumers have lost faith in brands and their ability to ignite social change: 41%, down five points from last year, believe brands have better ideas for solving a country's problems than government; 49%, down four points from last year, say brands can do more to solve social ills than government; and 48%, down six points from last year, feel it's easier for people to get brands to address social problems than to get government to take action.

"Consumers are wary that brands are 'trustwashing' and being less than truthful about their commitment to society," said Amanda Glasgow, global chair of Brand at Edelman. "Talking about an issue in an ad isn't enough. Brands need to go further to impact real change. This could be anything from advocacy to financial support to internal reforms."

Advertising alone is not enough, brands can build trust by communicating with consumers through various platforms and voices. While nearly three-quarters (74%) of respondents say they find ways to avoid advertising, our supplemental online influencer study found that a majority of consumers age 18-34 (63%) are more trusting of influencers than a brand's advertising. Repetition and specific sequencing of the brand message are also key.

More than three-fourths (87%) of respondents have strong trust in a brand message after seeing it across six different channels, compared to 13% who have strong trust in a message after just one viewing. The most effective channel sequence for building trust in a message among people who are not customers of the brand begins with peer conversation, amplified by owned (74%).

"It's time for brands to take the next giant step," said Edelman. "They must accept the responsibility consumers have given them to effect change and welcome greater accountability and measurement of their impact."

**SOURCE:** Edelman, International Square 1875 Eye Street, NW Suite 900, Washington, D.C. 20006

## Emoji Users Say They're More Likely to Engage With Brands That Use Emojis

Instagram posts that include at least one emoji have been found to generate more interaction than those without, making them a surprisingly useful engagement tool as opposed to just a way to dress up an otherwise dull message. So, how do consumers respond when brands use emojis in their messaging? A new study from Adobe looks at just that.

Adobe surveyed 1,000 U.S. emoji users ages 16-73 years old for the study, and half (51%) say they are more likely to engage with a brand's social media posts if they use emojis. They also like the personal touch, with 60% saying they like brands that use emojis that match their personality.

Emojis don't just inspire social media engagement. Close to half (48%) of respondents also say they are more likely to follow a brand on social media if it uses emojis, while 44% claim to be more likely to purchase products that are advertised using emojis.

Email is another area that can benefit from some well-placed emojis. GetResponse discovered that while very few businesses utilize emojis in their email subject lines, those that did had a slightly higher open rate than the emoji-free subject lines. Adobe's study backs up this finding, with 58% of respondents saying they are more likely to open an email with an emoji in the subject line.

More importantly, Adobe found that the emojis brands use in their subject lines also matter. Nearly two-thirds (64%) of respondents say they are more likely to open an email with their favorite emoji in the subject line. Broken down a bit further, three-quarters (75%) of Gen Z respondents say they are likely to open an email with their favorite emoji in the subject line compared to Millennials (63%), Gen Xers (59%) and Boomers (65%). (Overall, respondents' favorite emoji was the laughter emoji, followed by heart and kisses.)

Have you ever made a purchase using an emoji? Chances are, you haven't yet, but the study reveals that two-thirds (64%) of emoji users are willing to make a purchase using an emoji, with one-fifth (19%) saying they are most likely to purchase a meal at a restaurant or fast-casual spot via emoji. One such example is with pizza giant, Dominos, where after setting up a profile, customers can order through text by sending the pizza slice emoji.

Other respondents are willing to purchase movie tickets (15%), apparel (13%), accessories (8%) and sporting event tickets (7%) via emoji.

**Source:** Adobe, 345 Park Avenue, San Jose, CA 95110-2704, 408-536-6000

# Chapter 3

# College

## College Degree Widens Gender Earnings Gap

More education leads to higher earnings but the gender pay gap is wider among men and women with a bachelor's degree than among those without.

Among workers with a bachelor's degree, women earn 74 cents for every dollar men make, which is less than the 78 cents for workers without the college degree.

While workers with a bachelor's degree earn about double that of their co-workers without a college education, the difference between men's and women's earnings widens with more education.

Age and job choice can affect the size of the pay gap.

**Age**

Women workers with a bachelor's degree are younger on average and many are years away from the earnings peak usually reached by people in their 50s.

Higher pay reflects years of work experience and pay raises. The earnings differences between men and women also peak in their 50s, although men on average earn more at every age than their female counterparts.

Among workers with a bachelor's degree, women are considerably younger, on average, than men (median ages of 42 vs. 45). This results in a larger pay gap, as women have had less time to accumulate experience and pay raises.

In contrast, working women without a bachelor's degree are, on average, older than male workers without a bachelor's (median ages of 47 vs. 45), which tends to narrow the pay gap.

**Education**

At all ages in both education groups, men outnumber women except for the youngest age group (25-29) with a bachelor's degree.

The influx in recent decades of college-educated women has driven their numbers to record levels. In fact, the number of women working full time, year-round with a bachelor's degree is almost equal to men's (18 million women and 21 million men).

Women are more likely to have a bachelor's degree than men (41.7% compared with 36.2%) among full-time, year-round workers. This is particularly true for workers under age 60.

As older educated male workers age out of the labor force, this pattern of the college-educated workforce dominated by women may continue. Of note, male workers without a bachelor's degree make up the largest group by far.

**Jobs**

In some occupations, the earnings gap virtually disappears.

The mixture of the jobs men and women hold, and the earnings differences among these occupations, also contribute to the overall earnings gap.

**Among the highlights:**

- In many occupations, the earnings gap doesn't exist: phlebotomists, electricians, and social workers. This is particularly noticeable when accounting for educational attainment.

- Women and men workers concentrate in different occupations.

Among full-time, year-round workers, some of the largest occupations for women are secretaries and administrative assistants, registered nurses, and elementary and middle school teachers.

For men, the list includes driver/sales workers and truck drivers, first-line supervisors of retail sales workers, janitor and building cleaners, and construction laborers.

- All of the largest occupations with over 1 million full-time workers show some degree of earnings gap between men and women. This pattern remains for most of these occupations even when accounting for educational attainment.

- Occupations in which men are, on average, older than women have higher earnings on average, compared with occupations in which women are older.

- Selecting between the two educational attainment options shows a significant effect of more education on earnings for most occupations, for both men and women. It also displays a noticeable shift to a younger labor force, particularly for women.

**SOURCE:** U.S. Census Bureau, 4600 Silver Hill Rd, Suitland, MD 20746

## Recent Grads Give Themselves a 'C minus' in Personal Finance

A multitude of budgeting and money apps and extraordinary access to financial literacy materials haven't made too much of a difference, with more than half of today's high school and college graduates barely able to pass personal finance. A new study from Ally Bank shows that 53% of 18- to 24-year-olds say their personal finance knowledge is that of a C or lower.

A variety of topics are unveiled in the report including financial habits and behaviors as well as how consumers grade themselves on their knowledge of personal finance. The results show that adults ages 18-24 give themselves much lower grades than adults in general when it comes to personal finance, with only 1 in 10 saying they get an A.

"The ability to understand and manage your finances is often considered one of the keys in achieving a more secure life, however this survey illustrates that for some, they are still not comfortable navigating their own financial waters," said Diane Morais, president of Consumer and Commercial Banking Products for Ally Bank. "The good news is banks like Ally are here to help boost people's financial GPA with competitive products that make their money work harder. In addition, our online and mobile tools are simple to use and ideal to help them better manage their finances."

**Friends, Family Source for Knowledge, Not Schools**

Even with a bevy of ratings, reviews, and articles detailing a variety of personal financial tips, those 18-24 are twice as likely as older adults to learn from friends or family when it comes to personal finance. In fact, 18- to 24-year-olds are twice as likely to ask friends than use an online resource to learn more about personal finance.

But learning in an academic setting is trending up.

The study indicates that more recent high school graduates are three-times more likely to learn about personal finance during high school than older adults (23% to 7%). This may be driven by the fact that 60% of adults feel that personal finance should be taught in high school.

However, more than half (54%) say they would like to learn how to manage their finances better.

**Turn Back Time**

Ally also asked those who have celebrated their 10-year college reunion what advice they would give their college self. Avoiding student loans was high on the list of many of the respondents, as was understanding how best to use credit cards.

Other tips alums offered included:

- Set and stick to a budget
- Pay extra on debts like car loans or mortgages
- Save early as compounding interest pays off in the long run

**SOURCE:** Ally, 500 Woodward Ave, Detroit, MI 48226

# Chapter 4

# ENVIRONMENT

## Less Than 1 Million Bicycle to Work

May is National Bike Month, sponsored by the League of American Bicyclists and celebrated in communities from coast to coast. Established in 1956, National Bike Month is a chance to showcase the many benefits of bicycling — and encourage more folks to giving biking a try.

They've got a ways to go. According to the U.S. Census Bureau, about 837,000 workers in the U.S. bicycled to work in 2017 – the latest figures available from the Census Bureau -- down from about 865,000 in 2012 and up from 665,000 in 2007. Of those, 603,577 were male.

Compared to the number of workers driving to work – 130,340,856 – the number of bicyclists is a minuscule number.

**SOURCE:** Table B08006, Sex of Workers by Means of Transportation to Work, Universe: Workers 16 years and over, American Community Survey, 1 year estimates, U.S. Census Bureau.

## Most Americans Say They're Willing to Pay More For Environmentally Friendly Products

More than half (54%) of U.S. shoppers agree (43%) or strongly agree (11%) that they are willing to pay more for environmentally friendly products. This is according to a new issue of The Checkout by The Integer Group, who found that a willingness to pay a premium for "green" products has increased since the beginning of the decade.

In 2011, just one-third (24%) of shoppers were willing to pay more for green products, with most shoppers (43%) saying they were on the fence about paying more for environmentally friendly products. It should be noted that 2011 was the same year Gallup found that Americans' concern about environmental issues saw a decline.

Yet there now seems to be a larger emphasis on corporate responsibility, with consumers acting as advocates for companies that are both purpose-driven and show a commitment to the environment as well as society. Preventing climate change, clean water and wildlife preservation make shoppers more willing to purchase from brands.

Additionally, U.S. consumers appear more willing than they were in 2011 to recycle or reuse items they would have typically thrown away, as well as to purchase all-natural or organic products.

The green product respondents purchased most recently was most likely to be either perishable grocery items or cleaning items (each cited by 29% share of respondents). Roughly one-quarter (24%) pointed to household paper products as their most recent environmentally conscious purchase. When respondents were asked why they purchased their latest such product, half (51%) said that they were conscious about the environment while, surprisingly, one-third (33%) said it was to save money.

Other research has found that being an environmentally conscious shopper includes not only the actual product but also the packaging. A recently conducted survey from PwC found more consumers around the globe are now avoiding plastic, as well as purchasing products with either environmentally friendly packaging or less packaging altogether.

**SOURCE:** The Integer Group, 7245 West Alaska Drive, Lakewood, CO 80226

# Chapter 5

VZ
35.72
-0.31
Dow Jones
34,076.24
+14.92
S&P 500
4,359.71
+1.37
Dow Jones
Dow Jones Industrial Average
34,076.24 +1,224
Past Week
Dow Jones · USD
1D 1W 1M 3M 6M YTD 1Y 2Y
34,190
33,834
33,478
33,122
31 1 2 3 6
Open 34,092.61
High 34,167.26
Low 34,044.99
Vol 117.6M
P/E –
Mkt Cap –
52W H 35,679.13
52W L 31,429.82
Avg Vol 307.7M

# FINANCE

## U.S. News: One in Five Americans Don't Know Whether They Have Credit Card Debt

Almost a quarter (21%) of Americans don't know if they have credit card debt and 30% are unaware of how much interest they pay each month. This according to U.S. News & World Report, the global authority in rankings and consumer advice.

In its more recent survey, U.S. News discovered that nearly 25% of consumers in credit card debt owe more than $10,001. A number of consumers carrying a balance on one (37%) or two (27%) cards, with 12% of respondents carrying debt on five or more.

"When I was young, I fell into a sea of credit card debt because I was uneducated about personal finance and unaware of the high interest rates associated with credit cards," said Beverly Harzog, best-selling author, credit card expert and consumer finance analyst at U.S. News. "Luckily, there are tricks like balance transfers that allow consumers to pay off their debt while paying zero interest for a year or more. If you qualify, a balance transfer credit card can save you money and help you get back on track financially."

**Additional findings from the U.S. News & World Report survey:**

- **A tale of two extremes: Consumers have either little or extreme amounts of credit card debt.** Sixty percent of consumers do not have any credit card debt. Of those who do, 25% reported revolving credit card debt ranging from $1 to $2,000, while 24% reported more than $10,001 in credit card debt. What's more, 13% say credit card debt causes them to struggle to make ends meet, and 15% say their debt regularly limits their spending.

- **People think they can easily manage multiple cards.** Forty-nine percent of consumers do not find it difficult to manage multiple monthly payments. Only about 14% say it's moderately or very difficult.

- **Generally, consumers haven't taken advantage of balance transfers**. Almost half of respondents surveyed (48%) said they have never used a balance transfer offer. But 17% saved money on interest payments, and 12% paid off their balance before the offer ended.

- **Consumers are naive when it comes to potential fees.** Almost half of respondents (45%) didn't know whether their credit card charged a balance transfer fee.

**SOURCE:** U.S. News, 4 New York Plaza New York City, New York, 10004

## 30% Of Americans Are Within Three Paychecks Of Needing To Borrow Money Or Skip Paying One Or More Bills

Lack of savings paints a disconcerting picture about financial preparedness in America with almost a third (30%) of U.S. adults aged 18+ within three paychecks of needing to either borrow money or skip paying one or more bills. These are the latest findings from the 2019 Planning & Progress Study released today by Northwestern Mutual.

According to the study, more than a fifth (22%) of Americans have less than $5,000 saved for retirement, and nearly half of working adults (46%) expect to work past the traditional retirement age of 65.

"People are skating on some very thin ice financially," says Emily Holbrook, senior director of planning at Northwestern Mutual. "While there are some signs of improvement since last year we still have a long way to go, and for most Americans there's no way to get there without a plan."

The annual study found:

- More than one in five (22%) Americans have less than $5,000 saved for retirement, and 15% have no retirement savings at all. That's an improvement from 2018 when 31% had less than $5,000 saved and 21% had no retirement savings at all.

- While 10,000 Baby Boomers turn 65 every day, nearly one in five (17%) have less than $5,000 saved for retirement and 20% have less than $5,000 in personal savings. For Gen X, the numbers are greater -- 21% have less than $5,000 saved for retirement and 22% have less than $5,000 in personal savings.

- More than half (56%) of Americans don't know how much they'll need to retire comfortably.
- More than a fifth (22%) of non-retired U.S. adults believe it is not at all likely that Social Security will be available when they retire.
- On average, people think there is a 45% chance they will outlive their savings, and 41% have taken no steps to address it.

**When I'm 65...I'll Still Be Working**

The 2019 Planning & Progress Study found that 46% of Americans expect to work past the traditional retirement age of 65. Nearly one out of five Baby Boomers (18%) and an equal percentage of Generation X (18%) expect to work even longer -- past the age of 74.

Interestingly, more than half (53%) of Americans who expect to work past age 65 say it will be by choice, compared to 47% who say it will be out of necessity.

Among those who say they expect to work past age 65 out of necessity, the top three reasons why include:

- "I won't have enough saved to retire comfortably" (78%)
- "I do not feel like Social Security will take care of my needs" (56%)
- "I am concerned about rising costs like healthcare" (49%)

For those expecting to work past 65 by choice, the top three reasons why include:

- "I enjoy my job/career and would like to continue" (58%)
- "I want additional disposable income" (46%)
- "It is a social outlet that will help me stay active/prevent boredom" (39%)

"We're seeing a combination of factors in these numbers," says Holbrook. "Given what we know about savings levels, the number of people who can afford to retire at 65 is low. At the same time, people across the country are changing what the face of retirement looks like and getting satisfaction well beyond their bank accounts by continuing to work. The combination of those factors – affordability and lifestyle – form the bedrock of a good financial plan."

**An Interesting Juxtaposition**

The latest set of findings from the 2019 Planning & Progress Study are an interesting juxtaposition against the first set of data from the study released in May. Those results suggest that U.S. adults aged 35+ feel their financial habits and financial security have improved over the last 10 years, while risk aversion continues to run high, and optimism has remained flat. It's important to note that the sample used in the first set of findings – U.S. adults aged 35+ – is older than the sample used in this latest set of findings – U.S. adults aged 18+.

"Clearly it's not an apples-to-apples comparison between these first two sets of findings, but side-by-side they tell us two things," says Holbrook. "First, while middle-aged and older adults report improvement, they're still on a long road, just moving in a slightly better direction. Next, while there are some troubling signs about long-term financial security in America, there is also some evidence that as people age financial discipline becomes more of a priority."

**SOURCE:** Northwestern Mutual, 720 E Wisconsin Ave, Milwaukee, WI 53202

## 92% Of Americans Say Nothing Makes Them Happier Or More Confident Than When Their Finances Are In Order

Nearly all U.S adults aged 18+ (92%) agree that nothing makes them happier or more confident in life than when their finances are in order, this according to the latest findings from Northwestern Mutual's 2019 Planning & Progress Study.

While there is a link between financial stability and emotional well-being, most Americans have room for improvement where their finances are concerned. Despite some signs that behaviors are trending in the correct direction, a gap remains between intent and action:

- More than six out of 10 Americans (62%) say their financial planning needs improvement, which is down from the 70% who said the same in 2018

- 59% identify themselves as either disciplined or highly disciplined planners, which is an improvement over the 49% who said the same a year ago

- Those who say they don't plan at all is down to 11% in 2019, vs. 14% in 2018; 30% haven't spoken to anyone about financial planning, an improvement from the 34% who said the same a year ago. While 64% of Americans agree there are likely to be more financial crises in the future, 20% say their retirement / financial plan has not been created to endure ups and downs in the market

- Nearly half (48%) report they don't have clarity on how much they can afford to spend now vs. how much they should be saving for later

"We see something of a classic disconnect between theory and practice in these numbers," said Tim Gerend, executive vice president, career distribution. "While there is near unanimous acknowledgment that getting one's financial house in order is good for our mental health, breakdowns occur when it comes to taking action. That said, it's worth noting that some progress has been made year-over-year. Hopefully that's a trend that not only continues but accelerates."

**Advisor Usage Remains Low, but Benefits Run High**

Although Americans recognize that their financial planning efforts need improvement, few seek guidance from a financial professional. Only one-third (31%) of U.S. adults work with an advisor, which is flat to the proportion of the population who said the same last year.

However, the benefits of seeking professional help come across distinctly in the data. Those who work with advisors report substantially greater financial security, confidence and clarity than those who go it alone:

| U.S. Adults, Age 18+ | With | Without |
|---|---|---|
| Feel very financially secure | 66% | 31% |
| Feel as if they're headed in the right | 85% | 71% |
| Are happy with their life | 71% | 50% |
| Have clarity on balancing spending | 61% | 50% |
| Set specific goals for the next 5-10 | 81% | 67% |
| Are confident they will achieve their goals in the next 5-10 years | 68% | 55% |
| Have financial plans built to endure | 73% | 30% |

"Too often, people assume that advisors are for people who have either achieved a certain level of wealth or have a complex financial situation," said Gerend. "We remind people every day that the road to financial security starts with having a solid financial plan, and the road to a plan starts with having an advisor you trust who can give you the confidence you need to take action. The most important part is getting started, and it's never too early to do that."

**Source:** Northwestern Mutual, 720 E Wisconsin Ave, Milwaukee, WI 53202

## Americans' Summer Vacation Spending Expected to Hit Record $101.7 Billion in 2019

Americans are planning to spend more on their summer vacations this year than they have in at least a decade. Allianz Global Assistance's 11th annual Vacation Confidence Index estimates the total spend will cross the $100 billion mark for the third consecutive year in the index's history, amounting to $101,700,000,000.

Americans anticipated to spend an average of $2,037 on vacations this summer, topping $2,000 for the first time since 2010 when the survey started tracking spending, and marking a 5.2% increase over last year. According to the fifth-annual Global Travel Forecast from the Global Business Travel Association and Carlson Family Foundation, travel prices are expected to rise sharply in 2019 due to a growing global economy and rising oil prices.

Nearly half (42%) of Americans believe they will take a vacation this year, nearing its lowest point since 2013 when only 40% were confident they would take one. More than half of Americans who are not confident (52%) in taking a vacation this summer cited financial reasons, while another four in 10 of those with low confidence (38%) are restricted by time constraints, such as not being able to take time off from work or not wanting to take time off from work.

Just under half (49%) of Americans say they usually take an annual summer vacation, a three percentage point increase from 2018. Most likely to take a vacation are Gen Xers (ages 35-40), high income earners ($100K+) and those who think a vacation is important. Two in 10 Americans (21%) have taken a vacation in the past three months, while more than half of Americans (51%) last took a vacation more than a year ago.

In analyzing travelers' summer vacation spending habits, Allianz found that Americans are predicted to spend over 20% (23.2%) more than they did in 2010 where the average anticipated spend was $1,653.

"Summer vacation spending will hit record levels this year, with Americans planning to spend an average of more than $2,000 on their trip, according to our 11th annual Vacation Confidence Index," said Daniel Durazo, director of marketing and communications at Allianz Global Assistance USA. "This will bring total spending to a record $101 billion, a number which reflects the continued value that Americans place on their summer trips. As the amount spent on vacations continues to increase, it's even more important that consumers purchase travel insurance when they book their trip, in order to protect their travel investment and protect against costly medical emergencies while traveling."

The Vacation Confidence Index has been conducted each summer since 2009 by national polling firm Ipsos Public Affairs on behalf of Allianz Global Assistance USA. A vacation is defined as a leisure trip of at least a week to a place that is 100 miles or more from home.

**SOURCE:** Allianz Global Assistance, P.O. Box 71533, Richmond, VA 23255-1533

## Cheap Sleep: Survey Shows More Than A Quarter of Americans Spent $200 Or Less (Even Nothing!) On Their Mattress

Even with focus on improving sleep health on the rise, many Americans aren't spending much on the one piece of furniture that can help cultivate a good night's sleep.

Luxury bedmaker DUX recently released a survey that found one in 10 Americans spent less than $200 when buying their current mattress. Another 16% didn't spend anything at all. The survey was conducted online by The Harris Poll for DUX from June 18-20, 2019, among 2,060 U.S. adults, among whom 1,714 bought their current mattress.

DUX also found that a majority (82%) of those who purchased their current mattress spent under $500.

Price is a starting point taken into considering when buying a mattress but it isn't the only factor. Mattresses that are lower in price may use cheap parts, often all sourced from the same manufacturers in an effort to keep prices down. These range from poorly designed springs to padding and memory foam that quickly break down and lose their supportive features.

"So many factors come into play for getting a good night's rest, but there's no doubt your bed is a pivotal piece of that recipe," said Ed Curry, president of DUX North America. "Often, it's marketing that sells cheaper beds, not the actual comfort. At DUX, we focus on the design, material and craftsmanship because we know once someone sleeps on it, they'll immediately notice the difference."

The top-two most important factors for sleep quality are “support” (74%) and “long-lasting” (57%) among Americans.

"It's crazy to think many of us don't blink an eye at spending thousands on a piece of furniture we don't use nearly as often as our beds but laugh at the idea of spending more than $1,000 on a mattress," Curry said. "With more evidence showcasing the importance of quality sleep, we expect that trend to ultimately change as people realize how a top-end bed can truly impact their sleep and ultimately their well-being."

**Source:** DUXiana 1803 Fillmore St, San Francisco, CA 94115-3125

## 2 in 3 Millennials Have Credit Card Debt, More Than Double the Number Who Have Student Loans

Perhaps surprisingly, student loans aren’t the biggest factor in weighing down the finances of millennials — that belongs to credit card debt, this according to a new report from C ompareCards.com which found only 13% of millennial credit cardholders are completely debt-free. Across all generations, nearly one in four cardholders expect to die in debt, including those in wealthier households.

CompareCards surveyed more than 1,000 cardholders about their debts, from credit cards and auto loans to mortgages and student loans. Cardholders revealed their wide-ranging battles with debt, and many indicated they aren't optimistic about their ability to pay it off.

Key findings

- **Just 13% of millennial credit cardholders are debt-free,** slightly higher than the 11% of Gen Xers who said the same, but far less than the 29% of baby boomers without any debt.
- **67% of millennials report having credit card debt, while just 36% face student loan debt.**
- **About 1 in 4 cardholders across all generations think they'll die in debt.**
    - 25% of women think they'll never be debt-free, compared to 19% of men.
    - 16% of those who expect to die in debt have a household income surpassing $100,000.

- **Only 7% of cardholders with kids under 18 are debt-free,** compared to more than 20% of those with older children or no kids at all.
- **7 in 10 of those in credit card debt across all age groups have at least one other type of debt as well.**
- **On average, millennials with debt expect to be debt-free at age 49**, and they took on their oldest existing debt at 24.
    - **Gen Xers who owe expect to be debt-free at age 67**, and they took on their oldest existing debt at 30.
    - **Baby boomers with debt expect to be debt-free at age 81**, and they took on their oldest existing debt at age 49.

Most conversations around millennials and debt center around the nation's trillion-dollar student loan crisis, but the truth is, credit card debt is far more prevalent. With many millennials juggling student loan or car payments on top of credit card bills, it's no wonder some think they'll never be debt-free," said Matt Schulz, CompareCards Chief Industry Analyst. "Across all generations, it's shocking that nearly a quarter expect to die in debt. Viewing debt as a financial death sentence only makes matters worse, and those in debt should commit to action wherever and whenever possible. An extra $10 or $20 toward monthly debt payments can really make a difference in the long run, especially when coupled with reduced spending or a side gig."

**Source:** Compare Cards, Cigar Factory, 701 East Bay Street, Suite 414, Charleston, SC 29403

# Chapter 6

# Food/Beverage

## More than half of U.S. employees who typically eat lunch during work hours struggle to make it healthy

When it comes to employed Americans, more than half (56%) who typically eat lunch during work hours struggle to make it healthy, and more than three-quarters (77%) say they're more likely to make healthier decisions at other times of the day if they eat healthy at lunch. This according to a new survey from the American Heart

Association, the leading voluntary health organization devoted to a world of longer, healthier lives, and Aramark, the largest U.S. based food service company.

The survey was conducted online by The Harris Poll on behalf of the American Heart Association and Aramark as part of their joint initiative, Healthy for Life 20 By 20, among 907 employed U.S. adults aged 18 or older who say they typically eat lunch during work hours.

"Understanding what employees are eating for lunch on a typical workday and what factors influence their choices helps us develop strategies to improve dietary intake with multi-level approaches through food systems, communities and individuals," said Anne Thorndike, MD, MPH, vice chair of the American Heart Association's Nutrition Committee and associate professor at Harvard Medical School. "The finding that healthier food choices at work may impact food choices throughout the rest of the day presents a unique opportunity for the workplace to have a positive influence on not only the employee's health but also the health of the employee's family."

The survey of employed U.S. adults who typically eat lunch during work hours found that:

- **More than 9 in 10** (91%) **are interested in improving the healthfulness of their typical workday lunch** with employees under 40 more likely to be extremely/very interested compared to employees aged 40+ (65% vs. 55%).

- **More than 4 in 5** (82%) **agree that having healthy food options at work is important** to them and more than 2 in 3 (68%) value help from their employer in becoming healthier.

- **About 4 in 5** (79%) whose workplace has on-site cafeteria, food service or vending machines get food there at least some of the time.

- **Nearly 9 in 10** (86%) **prepare work lunches at home at least some of the time**, with women more likely to do so than men (91% vs. 82%).

- **When eating an unhealthy lunch, employees under age 40 are more likely to be impacted at least a little bit by cost** (91% vs. 79%) **and choices of their peers or coworkers** (75% vs. 50%) than employees aged 40+.

- **On a stressful day at work, about 1 in 3** (35%) **say their lunch is less healthy than a typical day**, with women more likely to say so than men (40%

vs 32%).

Motivated by its mission to enrich and nourish lives and its Healthy for Life 20 By 20 collaboration with the American Heart Association to improve the health of all Americans, Aramark launched a major plant-forward initiative to boost nutrition across its menus in colleges and universities, hospital cafés and workplace locations. The initiative has resulted in a 15% average reduction in calories, saturated fat and sodium, and significant increases in fruits, vegetables and whole grains across those dining location menus.

"Aramark and the American Heart Association are proud of our shared commitment to help millions of people lead healthier lives," says Dan Wainfan, vice president, Brand Health, Wellness and Nutrition at Aramark. "Through this survey, and as part of extensive consumer insights gained throughout our Healthy for Life 20 By 20 initiative, consumers are emphasizing that health and wellness is top of mind every day. While they don't always make a healthy choice, they always want delicious, healthy choices available—at work and at home."

While employees who typically eat lunch during work hour cite limited availability of healthy foods (43%) as having a great deal/quite a bit of impact on eating an unhealthy lunch, more of these employees cite convenience (60%) and taste preference (54%) as having a great deal/quite a bit of impact on choosing an unhealthy lunch.

"Improving the nutrition content and reducing calories of classic favorites and typically indulgent menu items helps. Having more plant-based options to choose from at home and on menus helps. But in the end, people still need to choose to eat healthier food. The good news is most people said they are interested in doing better," said Thorndike.

**Source:** The Harris Poll, 155 Corporate Woods, Rochester, NY 14623, (585) 272-8400

# Chapter 7

# Gaming

## When Millennials Aren't Gaming, They're Watching Gaming Content

While gamers may be seen as easy targets for ridicule, the gaming industry is nothing to scoff at with 2018 revenues reported at more than $43 billion. Millennials, in particular, are big gamers with a new study by Nielsen reporting that two-thirds of US Millennials play video games every month.

Past research has shown that gamers do not fall into the stereotypical characterization fed by popular media platforms like television. Millennial gamers are no different. Most (54%) are employed full-time and have an average household income of $58K. Many have children (46%) and are at least college-educated (43%). They are even paying for movie/TV (76%) and music (38%) streaming services.

While Millennials like to play video games, they also like to watch gaming content. Nielsen reports that 7 in 10 (71%) of Millennial gamers use platforms such as YouTube and Twitch to watch gaming video content and online videos about games. In fact, they spend almost 6 hours per week watching this type of content.

Not only that, these individuals are doing their part to support content creators, either through subscriptions (monthly fees paid to creators through the platform where their content is streamed or uploaded) or donations (one-time payments of any value paid to creators).

Millennials are more apt to support creators through donations (an average of $28.73 per month) than they are through subscriptions (average of $25.21 per month). Comparing the generations, Gen Z and Gen X tend to spend more on subscriptions ($28.64 and 29.93 respectively) than Millennials do. Note, these averages do not include those that do not spend anything on supporting creators.

Millennial gamers and their gaming viewing habits have not been lost on advertisers. PwC recently released figures which have video game advertising reaching $1.6 billion this year and growing to $1.9 billion by 2023, while e-sports streaming advertising is also expected to see growth at least through 2023. Additionally, Google research has shown that video and display ads have the highest viewability performance with game content.

**Source:** Nielsen, 85 Broad St, New York, NY 10004, (646) 654-5000

# Chapter 8

# Guns

## In U.S., Nearly Half Fear Being the Victim of a Mass Shooting

The two August mass shootings that took the lives of 31 people in one weekend has left Americans more worried about themselves or a member of their family being the victim of a mass shooting in its wake, even more than they were after two previous massacres. Right now, nearly half (48%) of U.S. adults are "very" or "somewhat" worried, compared with 39% in 2017 after one gunman killed 58 people in Las Vegas and 38% in 2015 after a San Bernardino shooter left 14 dead.

The most recent poll was conducted August 15-30, less than two weeks after back-to-back shootings in a 13-hour period — 9 people were killed in Dayton, Ohio and 22 were killed in a Walmart store in El Paso, Texas. The 2015 and 2017 polls were conducted in the immediate aftermath of the shootings; the latest readings may have been even higher had the poll happened closer to the shootings.

In total, 19% of U.S. adults are very worried, 29% are somewhat worried, 27% are not too worried and 25% are not worried at all about becoming the victim of a mass shooting. There are stark differences in the levels of worry between some demographic subgroups. Most notably, Democrats and Democratic-leaning independents, those who do not personally own a gun, women and younger adults are all significantly more worried than their counterparts.

Except for partisanship, worry among each of these groups has remained the same or increased since 2015. In 2015 when Barack Obama was president, Democrats were less worried than Republicans about being a victim of a mass shooting and Republicans were more worried. With President Donald Trump in the White House, those levels of worry have flipped.

At the moment, more than half of Democrats (64%) and 27% of Republicans are very or somewhat worried. In 2015, 46% of Republicans and 32% of Democrats registered the same degree of worry.

While women have consistently expressed greater worry than men about being the victim of a mass shooting in all three polls, men have also become more worried in the past two years. The 20-point gender gap on the issue is smaller than it was in 2017, but the same as in 2015. In 2015, 48% of women and 28% of men were at least somewhat worried.

**Few Measures Being Taken to Avoid Mass Shooting**

Despite Americans' heightened concern, few are taking any of four measures tested by Gallup to avoid being the victim of a mass shooting. These questions, asked for the first time in August, assessed whether Americans' concern about mass shootings has caused them to avoid public places like stores, restaurants or churches, avoided events with large crowds such as concerts, festivals or sporting events, purchased a gun or other weapon, or purchased special products to protect them in the event of a mass shooting.

The largest percentages doing any of these is 13% for purchasing a gun and 12% for avoiding events with large crowds.

About half as many say they have avoided stores or other public places (6%) or purchased protective products (6%). For the most part, these four precautions haven't even entered Americans' minds. Majorities say they have not thought about purchasing protective equipment (62%) or avoiding public places (56%).

Women are more likely than men to say they have avoided going to events where large crowds are present, 17% vs. 7%, but men are more likely to have purchased a gun or other weapon (16%) than women (10%).

Those who say they are very worried about being the victim of a mass shooting are much more likely than those who are less worried to say they avoid going to events with large crowds (30%) and they avoid going to public places (20%).

**Bottom Line**

Americans' level of worry that they or a family member will be the victim of a mass shooting is higher than it was after two previous mass shootings. Previous Gallup research has shown that Americans are more likely to mention guns or gun control as the most important problem facing the country in the immediate aftermath of prior mass shootings, and over time, that concern wanes. In Gallup's August update of the most important problem question, there was a similar spike in mentions of guns or gun control. The September update, out later this month, will tell if the issue remains a high priority for Americans or as usual, has dissipated over time.

Likewise, as further mass shootings continue to occur in the U.S., more Americans may begin to change their lifestyles to avoid becoming a victim. For now, though, most in the U.S. are not taking drastic measures.

**Source:** Megan Brenan, Gallup

## Health Care, Mass Shootings, 2020 Presidential Election Causing Americans Significant Stress, New Stress In America Survey Finds

The American Psychological Association (APA) has released this years *Stress in America* survey which found that healthcare, mass shootings and next years presidential election are causing Americans significant sources of stress.

The 2020 election was identified as a significant source of stress by more than half of U.S. adults (56%) — up from 52% in the months leading up to the 2016 presidential election.

According to this year's survey, around 7 in 10 adults (69%) say that health care is a significant source of stress — on par to the 71% who say mass shootings are a significant source of stress. Among adults who experience stress about health care at least sometimes (47%), the cost of health care is the most commonly cited source of that stress (64%).

Adults with private insurance (71%) are more likely than those with public insurance (53%) to say the cost of health care causes them stress. More than half of adults overall (55%) worry that they will not be able to pay for health care services they may need in the future.

Unsurprisingly, mass shootings are the most common source of stress cited by U.S. adults in 2019, with more than 7 in 10 adults (71%) saying mass shootings are a significant source of stress in their lives. This is a nine percentage point increase from 2018, when more than 6 in 10 adults (62%) said mass shootings were a significant source of stress.

Demographically, Hispanic adults are most likely to say mass shootings are a significant source of stress (84%), followed by black (79%), Asian (77%), Native American (71%) and white (66%) adults.

Stress related to climate change/global warming has increased significantly since last year (56% in 2019 vs. 51% in 2018). And more adults are reporting that widespread sexual harassment causes them stress today than said the same in 2018 (45% in 2019 vs. 39% in 2018).

"There is a lot of uncertainty in our world right now — from mass shootings to climate change. This year's survey shows us that more Americans are saying these issues are causing them stress," said Arthur C. Evans Jr., PhD, APA's chief executive officer. "Research shows us that over time, prolonged feelings of anxiety and stress can affect our overall physical and mental health. Psychologists can help people develop the tools that they need to better manage their stress."

Immigration is cited as a stressor by nearly half of adults (48%), with Hispanic adults most likely to identify it as a stressor (66%), followed by Asian (52%), Native American (48%), black (46%) and white (43%) adults.

Discrimination is another stressor that has become more prevalent in recent years (25% vs. 24% in 2018, 21% in 2017, 20% in 2016 and 20% in 2015).). In 2019, the majority of people of color (63%) say that discrimination has hindered them from having a full and productive life, with a similar proportion of LGBT adults (64%) expressing the same sentiment.

When looking at the responses of people of color, this year's results represent a significant increase from 2015, the last time this set of questions was asked, when less than half (49%) said that discrimination prevented them from having a full and productive life.

Additionally, U.S. adults report mixed feelings about the country's future. While fewer than 2 in 5 adults (38%) feel the country is on the path to being stronger than ever, nearly three-quarters (73%) feel hopeful about their future.

"This year's survey shows us that current events affect Americans differently, with people of color more likely to say they feel stressed about health care, immigration and discrimination," said Evans. "While these are important societal issues that need to be addressed, the results also reinforce the need to have more open conversations about the impact of stress and stress management, especially with groups that are experiencing high levels of stress."

While average reported stress levels remain constant compared with last year (4.9 in 2019 and 4.9 in 2018 on a scale of 1 to 10, where 1 is "little or no stress" and 10 is "a great deal of stress"), there continues to be a generational difference, with Gen Z adults reporting the highest average stress level (5.8), followed by Gen Xers (5.5), millennials (5.4), boomers (4.2) and older adults (3.0).

Among the stressors that the survey tracks each year, work (64%) and money (60%) continue to be the most commonly mentioned personal stressors. However, the economy is cited as a significant source of stress less frequently in 2019 than it was at its height in 2008 (46% in 2019 vs. 69% in 2008).

**Source:** The Harris Poll, 155 Corporate Woods,

# Chapter 9

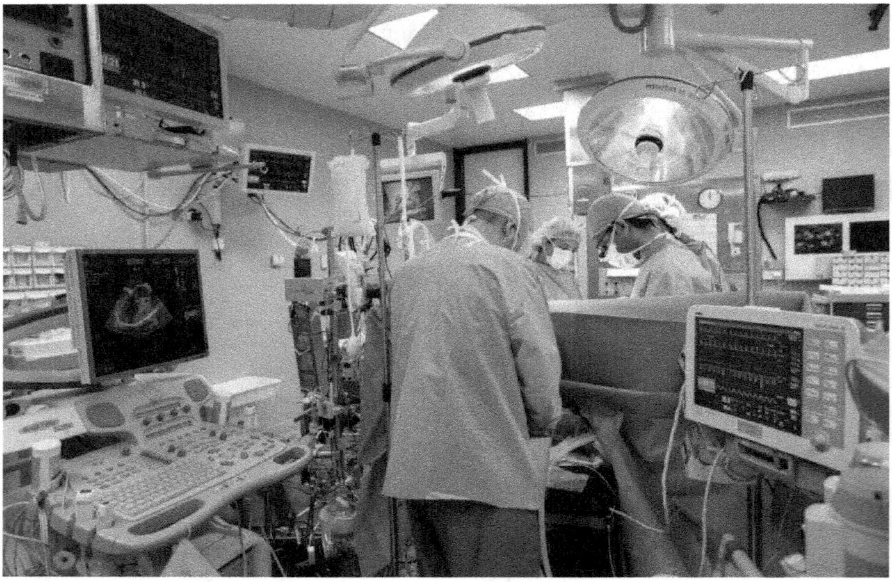

# HEALTHCARE

## Healthcare Costs Top Financial Problem for U.S. Families

When asked what the most important problem is facing their family, Americans are more likely to say healthcare costs than any other issue. Healthcare was named by 17%, followed by lack of money or low wages, named by 11%, this according to a new Gallup poll. Those two issues and personal debt tied for first a year ago, with healthcare also being the clear leading in 2017.

College expenses, housing costs and taxes follow as the problems mentioned next-most commonly in this year's survey, with 8% of Americans citing each.

The survey, conducted April 17-30, comes at a time of high economic confidence, when relatively few Americans name economic matters as the most important problem facing the country. Additionally, several different measures of Americans' personal financial situations are among the most positive Gallup has measured in years.

Twenty percent of Americans respond that they do not have a "most important financial problem" one of the highest percentages responding "none" in Gallup's 14-year trend on the question. It is surpassed only by the 21% who said so in February 2005.

Yet even in these generally good economic times, a majority of Americans do report that some financial matter is a concern for their family.

**Healthcare Costs Usually Near Top of the List**

Since 2005, Gallup has asked the "most important family financial problem" question nearly 50 times. In the 14 years of doing so only three issues – healthcare costs, energy costs/oil and gas prices and lack of money/low wages – have topped the list in any one poll.

The top problem before the Great Recession typically sees healthcare costs vying with energy costs, largely dependent on the price of gasoline. This included a record-high 29% mentioning gas prices in July 2008, when gasoline prices averaged over $4 per gallon nationwide.

Between 2009 and 2014 – periods of high unemployment and a sluggish economy recovery – lack of money or low wages was frequently the top personal financial problem. Since 2016, healthcare costs have ranked first in two of the surveys and been at least tied for first since 2014.

Over the last 14 years, an average of 8% of U.S. adults have named energy costs. Most frequently mentioned have been healthcare costs (14%) and lack of money (13%), the highest averages for any issues and the only two above 10%.

**Older Americans Especially Likely to Name Healthcare Costs as Top Problem**

The most commonly mentioned financial challenge is healthcare for key subgroups and is especially likely to be named by older Americans. With 25% of adults between the ages of 50 and 64, and 23% of those aged 65 and older, saying healthcare costs are the biggest problem for their family's finances.

Adults younger than 50 are about as likely to name lack of money, college expenses and housing costs with healthcare as their greatest financial challenges. Adults under 30 – the youngest adults – commonly mention debt and the high cost of living.

Those in pre-retirement years (aged 50 to 64) view retirement savings as a greater concern than young adults or senior citizens.

Americans at different income levels are about equally likely to name healthcare as the most important financial problem, with between 17% and 19% in each income group doing so. Not surprisingly, lack of money is a much greater concern for lower-income Americans. With upper- and middle-income Americans more likely to cite college expenses, taxes and retirement savings as their chief financial challenges.

**Implications**

Americans still face significant personal financial challenges, even in mostly good economic times, with healthcare costs being the top concern as well as consistent over time.

As such, healthcare will likely continue to be a major focus in national elections, including the 2020 presidential election. Older Americans, who are more likely to need healthcare and who are more likely to vote than younger Americans, may pay special attention to what the candidates' plans are for addressing healthcare costs.

**SOURCE:** Jeffrey Jones, Gallup

# Chapter 10

# HOLIDAY

## 1 in 3 Say Back-to-School Shopping More Stressful, Expensive Than Holiday Shopping

For millions of parents, back-to-school shopping is dreaded even more than holiday shopping, and about a third of shoppers said it's both more stressful and more expensive, according to a new report from CompareCards by LendingTree.

With the new school year fast approaching, CompareCards asked Americans about back-to-school shopping and found the end-of-summer ritual drives stress, debt and parent-child arguments – and many think their costs will only increase.

Key findings

- 36% think back-to-school shopping is more stressful than holiday shopping, and 32% said it's more expensive.
- 23% said back-to-school shopping has at least somewhat damaged their relationship with their child.
- More than a quarter of shoppers expect to go into debt because of back-to-school shopping, and most will not be able to pay off that debt quickly.
- Half of back-to-school shoppers plan to spend more this year than last year. On average, shoppers expect to spend $428 on back-to-school shopping this year.
- 43% are stressed about how they will pay for back-to-school shopping.

"With parents collectively spending billions of dollars on their children's back-to-school shopping needs each year, it's no wonder the end-of-summer ritual takes a toll on wallets, emotions and even relationships," said Matt Schulz, Chief Industry Analyst at CompareCards. "While it's unlikely shoppers can completely eliminate all stress from the back-to-school season, careful planning and savvy shopping goes a long way. Shoppers can set boundaries and budgets before heading to the mall, use credit card rewards and sign-up bonuses strategically, and comparison shop for the best deals. At the end of the day, back-to-school season happens just once per year, and soon enough the chaos will be over, so breathe, Mom and Dad. You've got this."

**Source:** LendingTree, 11115 Rushmore Drive, Charlotte, NC 28277

## Real Christmas Trees Make Real Family Memories

Real Christmas tree purchasers are more likely to place high importance on creating new holiday traditions with their families when compared with artificial tree users, a new survey reveals. In addition, the majority of real Christmas tree users incorporate a family tradition as part of their annual family outing to get a Christmas tree. The survey panel included 2,000 U.S. adults who celebrate Christmas and are parents of a child age 17 or under.

In fact, "keeping it real" by getting a real Christmas tree was cited as the top holiday activity that parents enjoyed when they were children, ranking above activities such as taking photos with Santa, cookie swaps, visiting extended family or going to the movies. Today, parents say they still enjoy the tradition of getting a Christmas tree with their children – second only to shopping for presents to put under the tree!

"Nothing says 'the holidays' like picking out a real Christmas tree with your loved ones, and this survey truly does confirm that real Christmas tree users are also the tradition keepers," said Marsha Gray, Executive Director, Christmas Tree Promotion Board. "From the unmistakable fresh Christmas tree scent to the fun of the search, the experience of choosing a real tree is a tradition to look forward to every holiday season and remember for years to come."

What else did the Christmas traditions survey uncover?

- **Dads Favor Tradition** – Dads were more likely to place a high importance on creating new holiday traditions with their children – including purchasing a real Christmas tree – when compared to moms.

- **Parents Pick the Tree** – When shopping for a real Christmas tree, 57 percent of parents say that they make the final call on the tree they'll take home, 31 percent let the kids do the selecting, 12 percent say they all pick together, and 5 percent say they rotate the big decision each year.

- **Mom Does the Tree Caretaking** – While dads enjoy tree traditions, they don't mind leaving the tree caretaking to mom, with 47 percent of moms doing the watering. Another 15 percent of parents said they assign the task to their kids while 15 percent said they all share in the duty as a family.

- **The More Lights the Merrier** – When it comes to decorating, 43 percent of parents said they prefer to adorn their tree with multi-colored lights, 21 percent prefer white lights, and 32 percent said they use both multi-colored and white lights.

**Source:** Christmas Tree Promotion Board, P.O. Box 77, Howell, MI 48844, 800-985-0773

# Chapter 11

# Housing

**Homes Get 3.4X More Views When Listed Than After Price Drop**

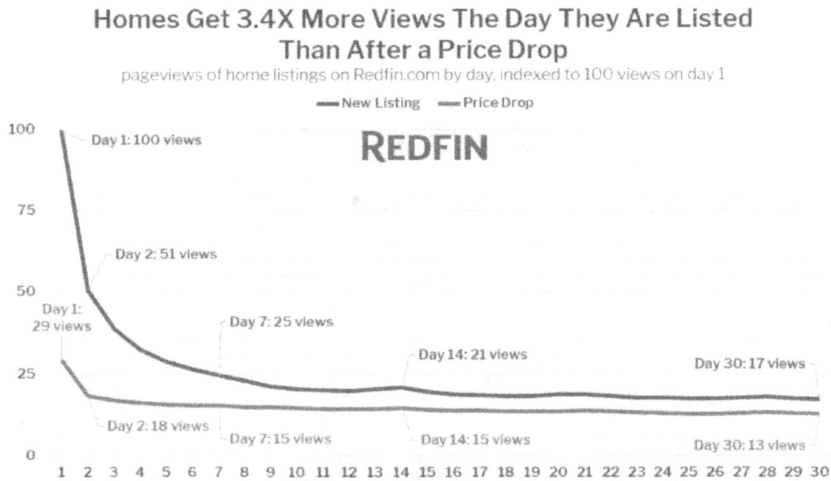

*CREDIT: Redfin Corp.*

Homes get 3.4 times more online views the day they are listed than they do the day the seller drops the price, according to a new report from Redfin, a technology-powered real estate brokerage.

The analysis looked at Redfin.com page views for more than 1.2 million listings and found the average number of views each listing received per day on the market, relative to the listing date and the date of the first price drop.

"It's critical to price your home to sell from the start," said Redfin chief economist Daryl Fairweather. "Fair or not, buyers judge a home by how many days it has been on the market. A home that has been on the market for more than a few weeks has a scarlet letter on it, and buyers will wonder why no one else wanted to buy it. Dropping the price can help get your home onto the radar of some buyers who are searching for homes priced just below the original price, but you likely won't be able to regain the appeal of a newly listed home."

A home for sale that is viewed by 100 buyers online in its first day receives an average of just 17 views per day after 30 days on the market. Dropping the price only boosts that to 29 views, and the bump only lasts a single day. The day after a price drop, the home's views fall back down to just 18 per day.

Online views of home listings drop off steeply after the first day, with half as many visits on day two and a quarter as many after a week on the market.

During the four-week period ending May 19, 24.2% of homes for sale had a price drop, up from 21% a year earlier, but down from the 30% record high posted last October. As home sellers this spring adjust to a market that's less favorable to them than it has been in years, it's increasingly important to make a home as appealing as possible to the most serious buyers, who often receive alerts when a home is first listed.

For this analysis Redfin collected Redfin.com page view counts of 1.2 million listings of homes for sale across the U.S. between January 2018 and March 2019 that had at least one price drop during the period. We averaged the number of views listings got each day on the market, relative to their listing date and the date of their first price drop. The data was indexed to 100 views on day 1 of the listing in order to clearly show the volume of listing views relative to day 1 of a new listing.

**SOURCE:** Redfin Corp. Data Center, Daryl Fairweather, 1-877-973-3346

## "Doorbells Before Wedding Bells" – New SunTrust Survey Finds Millennials Are Buying Homes on Their Own Terms

Just under half (48%) of millennials (ages 22-38) who have been married say they and/or their spouse owned a home before marriage, whereas only 35% of Baby Boomers (ages 55-73) did so. That's the conclusion of a new SunTrust Survey conducted online by The Harris Poll among more than 2,000 U.S. adults.

The survey found additional trends across generations:

**Putting Down New Roots** – unlike a few decades ago, today it is increasingly common for both parties in a relationship to own a property when entering a marriage. That being said, some individuals who are not married currently would still prefer to start fresh with their significant others and sell both properties prior to tying the knot. According to the survey, 25% of unmarried women and 21% of unmarried men said if faced with this decision, they would prefer to sell both places and buy a new one after getting married.

**Creature Comforts** – When it comes to motivations for buying their first house, millennials seem to have been driven by convenience more than their older counterparts. According to the survey, millennials who have owned homes were more likely than their older counterparts to cite proximity to work (29%, versus 18% of Gen X and 18% of Baby Boomers), schools (20% versus 12% and 10%), and leisure activities (16% versus 8% each) as primary motivators.

"It is easier to live life to the fullest – whether you are buying a home, downsizing, or selling – when you are financially confident. While everyone has different goals, across generations and lifestyle choices, it is important to make sure your financial habits are supporting, rather than preventing, the moments that matter most to you," Graziano said.

**SOURCE:** SunTrust Bank, 303 Peachtree St, Atlanta, GA 30308

# Chapter 12

# INTERNET

## 1 in Every 10 Adults in the U.S. Doesn't Use the Internet

The amount of U.S. adults who do not use the internet continues its slow decline, according to new data from Pew Research Center, with the percentage of the U.S. adult population who do not use the internet has more than halved in fewer than 10 years. Still, 1 in 10 U.S. adults remain non-internet users.

The new report finds similar patterns of internet usage seen in previous years, with adoption rates strongly correlating with age, household income, educational level, and community type.

It is worth noting that internet usage is consistent among me (90%) and women (90%).

However, despite figures from last year showing consistency among races and ethnicities, this year there is a larger gap in usage between White (92%), Black (85%), Hispanic (86%) adults.

**Age**

Research from AARP has shown that tech usage is regularly increasing among older Americans. However, internet usage remains the lowest among the oldest age group (65+).

Over one-quarter (27%) of adults ages 65 and older do not use the internet, according to the latest study. While this percentage has decreased from nearly one-third (34%) last year, it still means that less than three-quarters (73%) of the 65+ population is active on the internet and can be reached by digital means.

Although marketers are designating more of their digital marketing spend to target Baby Boomers, more traditional forms of marketing and advertising communications are still necessary to catch those adults refraining from online use. Traditional TV might be the best opportunity to reach these individuals since they have been shown to spend more time viewing traditional TV.

Meanwhile, roughly one in eight adults ages 50-64 (12%) do not go online. The percentage drops to 3% of 30-49-year-olds, and Pew's data shows that all 18-29-year-olds they surveyed use the internet.

**Household Income**

Nearly all adults with a household income of at least $50k use the internet, as do the vast majority (93%) of those with a household income of $30-50k. These figures have not changed from 2018.

That said, the number of non-internet users increases substantially among the lowest-income respondents, with 18% of those with a household income under $30K not on the internet.

Despite internet usage increasing over time for this group, it is doing so slowly; in 2013, almost one-quarter (24%) of those household income under $30K were not internet users.

**Educational Level**

Just like with household income, Pew's data sees a correlation between education levels and internet non-usage (i.e., the higher the level of education, the more likely to live a digital life). However, the difference is more noticeable.

Nearly three in 10 (29%) U.S. adults who have less than a high school education do not use the internet. Non-usage falls to 16% for those who obtained a high school diploma, and takes a drastic decline for those with some college (5%) and a college degree (2%).

**Community Type**

Adults who live in urban areas who don't go online increased to 9% this year from 8% last year. However, suburban adults have seen a significant decline in non-internet usage compared to 2018 (6% this year vs. 10% last year).

While a greater number of rural Americans do not use the internet compared to other communities, the number has also decreased in the past year to 15%, from 22%.

**SOURCE:** Pew Research Center, 1615 L Street, NW, Suite 800, Washington, DC 20036

# Chapter 13

# Jobs

## Women Win Promotions Sooner, But Hit Ceiling Sooner, Too

The average number of years for a woman to be promoted to her first manager position is 6.6 years. Men take a bit longer – 7.3 years — for the first step up the corporate ladder.

But each step up the ladder becomes harder for women, the study finds. As women move up management levels, there is a steep decline at the 3rd level of management; this decline becomes more pronounced at each level of advancement.

Managers are paid an average of $47 per hour, while non-managers earn $25.

Women earn $25 an hour, 79% of the $32 for males. The ratio of women pay to men reaches as high as 82% at the fourth level of management, but drops to 77% at the top levels of the firm.

Employees who have managers with more direct reports are more likely to leave the firm.

For example, direct reports' turnover for mangers with 4-6 direct reports is 2.3%; direct reports' turnover for managers with greater than 15 direct reports is 3.5%.

Leisure/Hospitality (11.4 direct reports) and Education/Healthcare (8.5 direct reports) have highest number of direct reports.

Firms are more likely to promote internally to management (17.2%) than make a new hire for management (15.6%)

At the highest level of management, 21.5% are internal promotions while just 12.5% are new hire.

The study is based on payroll data from more than 13 million employees.

Overall, employers promote 8.9% of their employees annually and those employees received an average wage increase of 17.4%.

Interestingly, however, promotions within a team are associated with higher turnover among other team members. Dr. Yildirmaz noted that, "While promotional opportunity may be perceived as a net positive, it can also have negative impact for team members who have been passed over." On the flipside, the probability for promotion exceeds 20 % for employees as they reach higher levels of management within the organization. Firms are more likely to promote internal employees for management positions, and the %age of internal hires increase for higher levels in the organization.

**SOURCE:** *ADP State of the Workforce Report: Pay, Promotions and Retention*, ADP Research Institute.

## College Degree Widens Gender Earnings Gap

More education leads to higher earnings but the gender pay gap is wider among men and women with a bachelor's degree than among those without.

Among workers with a bachelor's degree, women earn 74 cents for every dollar men make, which is less than the 78 cents for workers without the college degree.

While workers with a bachelor's degree earn about double that of their co-workers without a college education, the difference between men's and women's earnings widens with more education.

Age and job choice can affect the size of the pay gap.

**Age**

Women workers with a bachelor's degree are younger on average and many are years away from the earnings peak usually reached by people in their 50s.

Higher pay reflects years of work experience and pay raises. The earnings differences between men and women also peak in their 50s, although men on average earn more at every age than their female counterparts.

Among workers with a bachelor's degree, women are considerably younger, on average, than men (median ages of 42 vs. 45). This results in a larger pay gap, as women have had less time to accumulate experience and pay raises.

In contrast, working women without a bachelor's degree are, on average, older than male workers without a bachelor's (median ages of 47 vs. 45), which tends to narrow the pay gap.

**Education**

At all ages in both education groups, men outnumber women except for the youngest age group (25-29) with a bachelor's degree.

The influx in recent decades of college-educated women has driven their numbers to record levels. In fact, the number of women working full time, year-round with a bachelor's degree is almost equal to men's (18 million women and 21 million men).

Women are more likely to have a bachelor's degree than men (41.7% compared with 36.2%) among full-time, year-round workers. This is particularly true for workers under age 60.

As older educated male workers age out of the labor force, this pattern of the college-educated workforce dominated by women may continue. Of note, male workers without a bachelor's degree make up the largest group by far.

**Jobs**

In some occupations, the earnings gap virtually disappears.

The mixture of the jobs men and women hold, and the earnings differences among these occupations, also contribute to the overall earnings gap.

**Among the highlights:**

- In many occupations, the earnings gap doesn't exist: phlebotomists, electricians, and social workers. This is particularly noticeable when accounting for educational attainment.

- Women and men workers concentrate in different occupations.

Among full-time, year-round workers, some of the largest occupations for women are secretaries and administrative assistants, registered nurses, and elementary and middle school teachers.

For men, the list includes driver/sales workers and truck drivers, first-line supervisors of retail sales workers, janitor and building cleaners, and construction laborers.

- All of the largest occupations with over 1 million full-time workers show some degree of earnings gap between men and women. This pattern remains for most of these occupations even when accounting for educational attainment.

- Occupations in which men are, on average, older than women have higher earnings on average, compared with occupations in which women are older.

- Selecting between the two educational attainment options shows a significant effect of more education on earnings for most occupations, for both men and women. It also displays a noticeable shift to a younger labor force, particularly for women.

**SOURCE:** U.S. Census Bureau, 4600 Silver Hill Rd, Suitland, MD 20746

## Half of Employed Adults Likely to Job Hunt Next Year

Almost half of adults in the U.S. (48%) who are currently employed are likely to look for a new job in the next year, this according to the results of the latest American Staffing Association Workforce Monitor survey conducted online by The Harris Poll.

This includes transitioning to an entirely new career, not just finding a new job. Four in 10 adults currently working (38%) say they are likely to change careers (e.g., switch to a new industry or field, or a different position or role) within the next year, as do one in two Millennials (51%) and one in three members of Gen X (34%).

Many do not believe that landing their ideal job is a future possibility, as four in 10 working adults (44%) are worried they will never find the perfect job for them. Opinions differ based on employee occupation. Notably, half of those working in the office–administrative (51%), industrial (48%), and professional–managerial (47%) industry sectors lack confidence that they will ever find their ideal job, while one in four in health care (39%) and one in three in the engineering, IT, and scientific sector (32%) share this concern. And seven in 10 students (69%) also worry about finding the right job.

"The U.S. is immersed in the tightest labor market in modern history with millions of unfilled openings across geographies and industries," said Richard Wahlquist, ASA president and chief executive officer. "It's a job seeker's market—a reality lost on many people who, as the ASA Workforce Monitor shows, sadly lack optimism about their prospects of finding a perfect position."

**Source:** The Harris Poll, 155 Corporate Woods, Rochester, NY 14623, (585) 272-8400

# Chapter 14

# MARRIAGE

### "Doorbells Before Wedding Bells" – New SunTrust Survey Finds Millennials Are Buying Homes on Their Own Terms

Just under half (48%) of millennials (ages 22-38) who have been married say they and/or their spouse owned a home before marriage, whereas only 35% of Baby Boomers (ages 55-73) did so. That's the conclusion of a new SunTrust Survey conducted online by The Harris Poll among more than 2,000 U.S. adults.

The survey found additional trends across generations:

**Putting Down New Roots** – unlike a few decades ago, today it is increasingly common for both parties in a relationship to own a property when entering a marriage. That being said, some individuals who are not married currently would still prefer to start fresh with their significant others and sell both properties prior to tying the knot. According to the survey, 25% of unmarried women and 21% of unmarried men said if faced with this decision, they would prefer to sell both places and buy a new one after getting married.

**Creature Comforts** – When it comes to motivations for buying their first house, millennials seem to have been driven by convenience more than their older counterparts. According to the survey, millennials who have owned homes were more likely than their older counterparts to cite proximity to work (29%, versus 18% of Gen X and 18% of Baby Boomers), schools (20% versus 12% and 10%), and leisure activities (16% versus 8% each) as primary motivators.

"It is easier to live life to the fullest – whether you are buying a home, downsizing, or selling – when you are financially confident. While everyone has different goals, across generations and lifestyle choices, it is important to make sure your financial habits are supporting, rather than preventing, the moments that matter most to you," Graziano said.

**SOURCE:** SunTrust Bank, 303 Peachtree St, Atlanta, GA 30308

## Forty-Five Percent of Newlyweds Went into Debt for Their Wedding — and It's Causing Marital Problems

Almost half (45%) of newlyweds between the ages of 18 and 53 went into debt to pay for their wedding. And once married, nearly half of the newlyweds who obtained wedding-related debt said money has caused them to consider divorce. On the flip side, only 9% of couples without wedding-related debt contemplate divorce, this according to LendingTree's study on newlyweds and wedding expenses.

Key survey findings:

- 45% of Americans ages 18 to 53 who were married within the last two years went into debt for their wedding.

- 76% of newlyweds who went into debt for their wedding say they argued about wedding-related expenses with their partner. Comparatively, only 20% of those who avoided wedding debt said the same.

- Nearly half (47%) of newlyweds who went into wedding debt say money caused them to contemplate divorce, compared to just 9% of couples who did not go into debt for their wedding.
- 36% of those who had wedding debt say they argue with their partner about money often, versus 11% of couples without wedding debt.
- 1 in 4 newlyweds wish they spent less on their wedding, and their biggest regret was spending too much on food and drink or the venue.
- For about a third of newlyweds (32%), family caused the most headaches during the wedding planning process. Money was the primary stressor for 28%, and 17% reported the guest list as their biggest headache.

**SOURCE:** LendingTree, 11115 Rushmore Drive, Charlotte, NC 28277

# Chapter 15

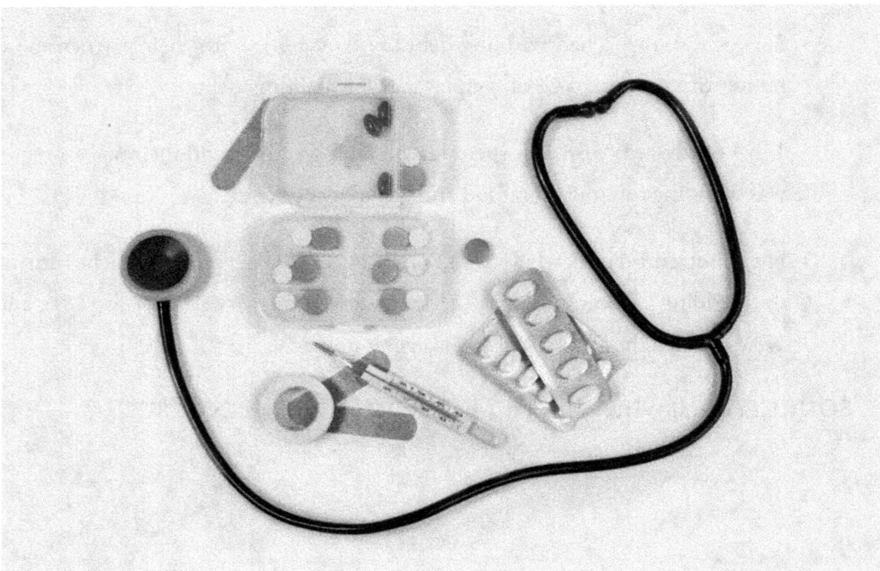

# MEDICAL

## 45% of American Adults Doubt Vaccine Safety, According to Survey

An online survey of more than 2,000 U.S. adults recently conducted by The Harris Poll on behalf of the American Osteopathic Association, revealed that more than two in five American adults (45%) say something has caused them to doubt vaccine safety.

The spread of negative attitudes towards vaccines is a phenomenon deeply rooted in human psychology and amplified by social media, according to perinatal psychiatrist Rachel Shmuts, DO.

"From an evolutionary perspective, humans are primed to pay attention to threats or negative information," she says. "So it makes sense that people hold onto fears that vaccines are harmful, especially when they believe their children are in danger."

Because vaccines have been so effective at reducing or eradicating diseases, she believes that some people may have more fear about possible side effects from the vaccines than the actual diseases the vaccines prevent.

"For some, it really might be that vaccines are viewed as the more salient threat," says Dr. Shmuts.

While more than half of Americans (55%) don't doubt vaccine safety, 45% acknowledged at least one source that caused doubts about vaccination safety. Online articles (16%), past secrets/wrongdoing by the pharmaceutical industry (16%) and information from medical experts (12%) are rank as the top three doubt-causing sources.

**No more room for doubt.**

Americans were also asked in the survey to choose a statement that best represented their feelings about vaccine safety and efficacy. While the vast majority (82%) chose in favor of vaccines, 8% selected responses expressing serious doubt. An additional 9% said they were unsure.

Physicians say those small margins can cause significant damage to public health if the doubts result in more unvaccinated people.

"Some diseases, like measles, require as much as 95% of the population to be vaccinated in order to achieve herd immunity," says osteopathic family physician Paul Ehrmann, DO. "Our practice considers itself a steward of public health, so we do not take new patients who refuse to vaccinate."

Dr. Ehrmann explains that herd immunity is essential to maintain, because some people cannot be vaccinated due to medical conditions including allergies, illness, or a weakened immune system. Keeping the rest of the population vaccinated protects those who are vulnerable.

"People know that a lot of practices won't accept patients who don't vaccinate, so when they find one that will, they spread the word to their community that it's a safe place. Whether intentional or not, those doctors are often seen as endorsing anti-vaxxer beliefs," Dr. Ehrmann said.

**Winning patients back**

While social media has helped spread misinformation about vaccines, it has not been effective for countering those claims, even with scientific research, according to Dr. Shmuts.

She explains that confirmation bias—the tendency to trust new information that bolsters existing beliefs and discredit information that challenges those beliefs—makes it difficult to convince someone vaccines are safe, effective and necessary once they believe they are not.

"The number of people who believe vaccines are dangerous and refuse to get them is still relatively small. However, online support groups seem to solidify their beliefs, making them less susceptible to influence from their neighbors and real-world communities," says Dr. Shmuts.

Dr. Ehrmann agrees, adding that arguing or being judgmental with patients only pushes them further into communities that share their beliefs. Instead, he thinks policy changes are likely the most effective means to change behaviors, if not hearts and minds.

His home state of Michigan discontinued public education for vaccines in the mid-2000s and allows for medical, religious and philosophical exemptions for vaccination, making the state accommodating to anti-vaxxers. As recent as 2015, Michigan ranked 44th in the country for the number of vaccinated children 19 months to 35 months.

However, in 2017 the state, with other partners, launched a public information campaign that has significantly improved vaccination rates across demographics.

"Beliefs are hard to change especially when they're based in fear," says Dr. Ehrmann. "But, being responsible for our patients' health and the public's health, we can't afford to give in to those fears. We must insist on evidence-based medicine."

**SOURCE:** American Osteopathic Association, 142 E. Ontario St., Chicago, IL 60611-2864, Phone: (888) 62-MYAOA (888-626-9262)

# Chapter 16

# MILLENNIALS

## "Doorbells Before Wedding Bells" – New SunTrust Survey Finds Millennials Are Buying Homes on Their Own Terms

Just under half (48%) of millennials (ages 22-38) who have been married say they and/or their spouse owned a home before marriage, whereas only 35% of Baby Boomers (ages 55-73) did so. That's the conclusion of a new SunTrust Survey conducted online by The Harris Poll among more than 2,000 U.S. adults.

The survey found additional trends across generations:

**Putting Down New Roots** – unlike a few decades ago, today it is increasingly common for both parties in a relationship to own a property when entering a marriage. That being said, some individuals who are not married currently would still prefer to start fresh with their significant others and sell both properties prior to tying the knot. According to the survey, 25% of unmarried women and 21% of unmarried men said if faced with this decision, they would prefer to sell both places and buy a new one after getting married.

**Creature Comforts** – When it comes to motivations for buying their first house, millennials seem to have been driven by convenience more than their older counterparts. According to the survey, millennials who have owned homes were more likely than their older counterparts to cite proximity to work (29%, versus 18% of Gen X and 18% of Baby Boomers), schools (20% versus 12% and 10%), and leisure activities (16% versus 8% each) as primary motivators.

"It is easier to live life to the fullest – whether you are buying a home, downsizing, or selling – when you are financially confident. While everyone has different goals, across generations and lifestyle choices, it is important to make sure your financial habits are supporting, rather than preventing, the moments that matter most to you," Graziano said.

**SOURCE:** SunTrust Bank, 303 Peachtree St, Atlanta, GA 30308

## When Millennials Aren't Gaming, They're Watching Gaming Content

While gamers may be seen as easy targets for ridicule, the gaming industry is nothing to scoff at with 2018 revenues reported at more than $43 billion. Millennials, in particular, are big gamers with a new study by Nielsen reporting that two-thirds of US Millennials play video games every month.

Past research has shown that gamers do not fall into the stereotypical characterization fed by popular media platforms like television. Millennial gamers are no different. Most (54%) are employed full-time and have an average household income of $58K. Many have children (46%) and are at least college-educated (43%). They are even paying for movie/TV (76%) and music (38%) streaming services.

While Millennials like to play video games, they also like to watch gaming content. Nielsen reports that 7 in 10 (71%) of Millennial gamers use platforms such as YouTube and Twitch to watch gaming video content and online videos about games. In fact, they spend almost 6 hours per week watching this type of content.

Not only that, these individuals are doing their part to support content creators, either through subscriptions (monthly fees paid to creators through the platform where their content is streamed or uploaded) or donations (one-time payments of any value paid to creators).

Millennials are more apt to support creators through donations (an average of $28.73 per month) than they are through subscriptions (average of $25.21 per month). Comparing the generations, Gen Z and Gen X tend to spend more on subscriptions ($28.64 and 29.93 respectively) than Millennials do. Note, these averages do not include those that do not spend anything on supporting creators.

Millennial gamers and their gaming viewing habits have not been lost on advertisers. PwC recently released figures which have video game advertising reaching $1.6 billion this year and growing to $1.9 billion by 2023, while e-sports streaming advertising is also expected to see growth at least through 2023. Additionally, Google research has shown that video and display ads have the highest viewability performance with game content.

**Source:** Nielsen, 85 Broad St, New York, NY 10004, (646) 654-5000

## 2 in 3 Millennials Have Credit Card Debt, More Than Double the Number Who Have Student Loans

Perhaps surprisingly, student loans aren't the biggest factor in weighing down the finances of millennials — that belongs to credit card debt, this according to a new report from C ompareCards.com which found only 13% of millennial credit cardholders are completely debt-free. Across all generations, nearly one in four cardholders expect to die in debt, including those in wealthier households.

CompareCards surveyed more than 1,000 cardholders about their debts, from credit cards and auto loans to mortgages and student loans. Cardholders revealed their wide-ranging battles with debt, and many indicated they aren't optimistic about their ability to pay it off.

Key findings

- **Just 13% of millennial credit cardholders are debt-free,** slightly higher than the 11% of Gen Xers who said the same, but far less than the 29% of baby boomers without any debt.
- **67% of millennials report having credit card debt, while just 36% face student loan debt.**
- **About 1 in 4 cardholders across all generations think they'll die in debt.**
    - 25% of women think they'll never be debt-free, compared to 19% of men.
    - 16% of those who expect to die in debt have a household income surpassing $100,000.
- **Only 7% of cardholders with kids under 18 are debt-free,** compared to more than 20% of those with older children or no kids at all.
- **7 in 10 of those in credit card debt across all age groups have at least one other type of debt as well.**
- **On average, millennials with debt expect to be debt-free at age 49**, and they took on their oldest existing debt at 24.

- **Gen Xers who owe expect to be debt-free at age 67**, and they took on their oldest existing debt at 30.

- **Baby boomers with debt expect to be debt-free at age 81**, and they took on their oldest existing debt at age 49.

Most conversations around millennials and debt center around the nation's trillion-dollar student loan crisis, but the truth is, credit card debt is far more prevalent. With many millennials juggling student loan or car payments on top of credit card bills, it's no wonder some think they'll never be debt-free," said Matt Schulz, CompareCards Chief Industry Analyst. "Across all generations, it's shocking that nearly a quarter expect to die in debt. Viewing debt as a financial death sentence only makes matters worse, and those in debt should commit to action wherever and whenever possible. An extra $10 or $20 toward monthly debt payments can really make a difference in the long run, especially when coupled with reduced spending or a side gig."

**Source:** Compare Cards, Cigar Factory, 701 East Bay Street, Suite 414, Charleston, SC 29403

# Chapter 17

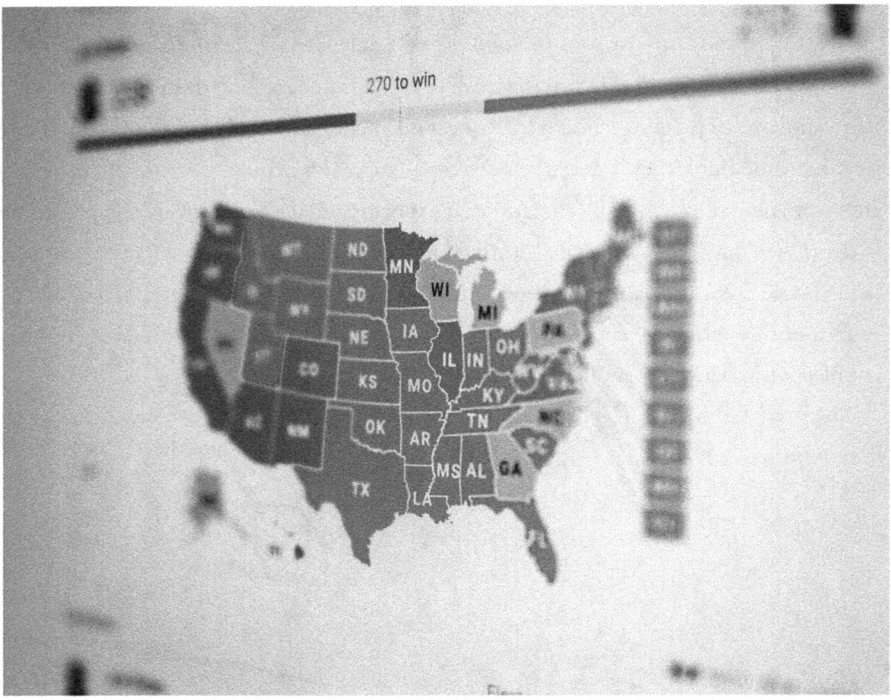


# POLITICS

## University of Phoenix: Half of U.S. Adults Can Define the True Meaning of Memorial Day

Memorial Day means the unofficial start of summer for many Americans. With a three-day weekend of backyard barbeques, beach trips, and holiday sales, Memorial Day Weekend (or MDW) can be a much-needed vacation or chance to unwind with friends and family, but the intended purpose is to honor military members who gave their life serving in the United States Armed Forces. And many adults are losing sight of the true meaning of Memorial Day, according to a recent survey from the University of Phoenix.

According to the survey, just 55% of respondents described Memorial Day as a holiday honoring the men and women who died serving in the U.S. Armed Forces.

Americans most often confused Memorial Day with Veterans Day, a holiday to thank living veterans for their service, with more than a quarter (27%) describing Memorial Day as a holiday honoring *all* military veterans.

"While most Americans recognize that Memorial Day is a military holiday, it is important to understand that it is a solemn day of remembrance. For me, as a combat veteran, and for military members and their families, this day holds great significance. Not everyone I served with was fortunate enough to return home," said Brian Ishmael, senior director, University of Phoenix Office of Military and Veteran Affairs and former U.S. Army sergeant. "We should enjoy Memorial Day, but we must also ensure that future generations understand and remember the sacrifices made protecting our freedoms."

The meaning of Memorial Day may be slowly eroding with each passing generation, despite most Americans having ties to the military additional findings show. More than three in five (63%) U.S. adults have themselves or have immediate family members who served in the U.S. Armed Forces.

However, only 46% of adults aged 18-34 identified the correct meaning of Memorial Day versus 58% of 45- to 64-year-olds. Adults aged 65 and over were most likely to cite it as a day of honoring those who died serving in the Armed Forces (65%).

**SOURCE:** University of Phoenix, 4025 S. Riverpoint Parkway, Phoenix, AZ 85040

## Health Care, Mass Shootings, 2020 Presidential Election Causing Americans Significant Stress, New Stress In America Survey Finds

The American Psychological Association (APA) has released this years *Stress in America* survey which found that healthcare, mass shootings and next years presidential election are causing Americans significant sources of stress.

The 2020 election was identified as a significant source of stress by more than half of U.S. adults (56%) — up from 52% in the months leading up to the 2016 presidential election.

According to this year's survey, around 7 in 10 adults (69%) say that health care is a significant source of stress — on par to the 71% who say mass shootings are a significant source of stress. Among adults who experience stress about health care at least sometimes (47%), the cost of health care is the most commonly cited source of that stress (64%).

Adults with private insurance (71%) are more likely than those with public insurance (53%) to say the cost of health care causes them stress. More than half of adults overall (55%) worry that they will not be able to pay for health care services they may need in the future.

Unsurprisingly, mass shootings are the most common source of stress cited by U.S. adults in 2019, with more than 7 in 10 adults (71%) saying mass shootings are a significant source of stress in their lives. This is a nine percentage point increase from 2018, when more than 6 in 10 adults (62%) said mass shootings were a significant source of stress.

Demographically, Hispanic adults are most likely to say mass shootings are a significant source of stress (84%), followed by black (79%), Asian (77%), Native American (71%) and white (66%) adults.

Stress related to climate change/global warming has increased significantly since last year (56% in 2019 vs. 51% in 2018). And more adults are reporting that widespread sexual harassment causes them stress today than said the same in 2018 (45% in 2019 vs. 39% in 2018).

"There is a lot of uncertainty in our world right now — from mass shootings to climate change. This year's survey shows us that more Americans are saying these issues are causing them stress," said Arthur C. Evans Jr., PhD, APA's chief executive officer. "Research shows us that over time, prolonged feelings of anxiety and stress can affect our overall physical and mental health. Psychologists can help people develop the tools that they need to better manage their stress."

Immigration is cited as a stressor by nearly half of adults (48%), with Hispanic adults most likely to identify it as a stressor (66%), followed by Asian (52%), Native American (48%), black (46%) and white (43%) adults.

Discrimination is another stressor that has become more prevalent in recent years (25% vs. 24% in 2018, 21% in 2017, 20% in 2016 and 20% in 2015).). In 2019, the majority of people of color (63%) say that discrimination has hindered them from having a full and productive life, with a similar proportion of LGBT adults (64%) expressing the same sentiment.

When looking at the responses of people of color, this year's results represent a significant increase from 2015, the last time this set of questions was asked, when less than half (49%) said that discrimination prevented them from having a full and productive life.

Additionally, U.S. adults report mixed feelings about the country's future. While fewer than 2 in 5 adults (38%) feel the country is on the path to being stronger than ever, nearly three-quarters (73%) feel hopeful about their future.

"This year's survey shows us that current events affect Americans differently, with people of color more likely to say they feel stressed about health care, immigration and discrimination," said Evans. "While these are important societal issues that need to be addressed, the results also reinforce the need to have more open conversations about the impact of stress and stress management, especially with groups that are experiencing high levels of stress."

While average reported stress levels remain constant compared with last year (4.9 in 2019 and 4.9 in 2018 on a scale of 1 to 10, where 1 is "little or no stress" and 10 is "a great deal of stress"), there continues to be a generational difference, with Gen Z adults reporting the highest average stress level (5.8), followed by Gen Xers (5.5), millennials (5.4), boomers (4.2) and older adults (3.0).

Among the stressors that the survey tracks each year, work (64%) and money (60%) continue to be the most commonly mentioned personal stressors. However, the economy is cited as a significant source of stress less frequently in 2019 than it was at its height in 2008 (46% in 2019 vs. 69% in 2008).

**Source:** The Harris Poll, 155 Corporate Woods,

# Chapter 18

# RETAILERS

## Consumers First Hear About New Retailers Through Friends and Family

For nearly half of consumers (45%), the first time they hear about a retailer they've never purchased from is through friends and family, according to a new study by Yes Marketing.

In "The Retail Shopper's Journey to Loyalty," Yes Marketing surveyed over 1,000 retail shoppers and found that word-of-mouth recommendations significantly outweighed other sources, including product review sites (8%), influencer recommendations (4%) and news sites (2%) when it comes to driving brand awareness. Nearly three-fourths (69%) of consumers have avoided shopping with a retailer they've never purchased from before because of negative feedback from family or friends. The findings indicate that building trust and goodwill with customers early on is crucial for marketers.

The report found that comprehensive product information and message relevance are among the top factors that build trust with a new retailer. More than a third of consumers (36%) reported that having enough product information is the number one driver of trust in retailers they've never shopped with before.

"Building trust is key at the acquisition and retention stages of the shopper's journey," said Jim Sturm, CEO of Yes Marketing. "To win over skeptical customers, retailers must convince consumers that their products are valuable and that their brand is trustworthy, especially in industries like luxury goods, home furnishings and electronics where the price tag is higher and consumers purchase less frequently."

In terms of the products themselves, almost half (47%) of consumers ranked price as the most influential factor in their decision to purchase from a new retailer, followed closely by quality (39%), indicating an opportunity for marketers to emphasize these elements in communications with new prospective customers. Additionally, when it comes to convenience, 40% of consumers rank shipping as the number one factor in their decision to purchase from a new retailer.

"The number of retail options consumers can choose from has sky-rocketed in recent years, and in order to survive in today's competitive landscape retailers must implement effective lifecycle strategies at every stage of the consumer journey – from acquisition and retention to long-term loyalty," said Michael Iaccarino, CEO and chairman of Infogroup, parent company of Yes Marketing. "Successful lifecycle programs that identify and engage consumers require a partner with a wealth of strategic, analytics and creative experience, access to reliable consumer data and proven technical expertise."

Additional findings from the report include:

- A third of consumers (33%) say relevant brand messaging is the most influential marketing factor when choosing to purchase from a retailer for the first time.

- Nearly a quarter of consumers (24%) say proximity to a store is the most influential convenience factor when choosing to purchase from a retailer for the first time.

- Across channels, 32% of consumers say they receive marketing messages too frequently from retailers they've purchased with, and more than a third (36%) say they receive too many emails.

- Conversely, 7% of consumers say they receive marketing messages too infrequently from retailers they've purchased with.

**SOURCE:** Yes Marketing, 200 W Adams St., Suite 1400, Chicago IL, 60606

# Chapter 19

# SCHOOL

## Gadgets Advance to the Head of the Class This Back-to-School Shopping Season

Spending for back-to-school is anticipated to reach $27.8 billion, averaging $519 per student in households buying clothes, supplies, computers and electronics for children in grades K to 12, this according to Deloitte's annual Back-to-School Survey.

Spending on electronics and gadgets (smartphones, tablets, wearables) are set to rise $800 million, a 29% increase over 2018. Consumers planning to purchase these items (22%) intend to spend an average of $305 on them.

Consistent with prior years, the majority of back-to-school purchases will occur in stores (56%), but online is gaining ground and looks to grab around 29% of back-to-school spending — up from 23% last year. The increase reflects a shift online among individuals who were previously undecided between online and in-store.

Use of personal computers overall for back-to-school shopping is down from 49% in 2018 to 42% in 2019, while 60% are reaching for their smartphones this year, primarily to visit a retailer's website (54%), obtain price information (51%) and look for discounts/promotions (51%).

"For the first time, people are telling us they're just as likely to use a smartphone to make purchases as a laptop or desktop, which previously held the lead when it was time to click the 'buy' button," said Rod Sides, vice chairman, Deloitte LLP and U.S. retail, wholesale and distribution leader. "Additionally, we continue to see just over half of purchases occurring in the stores, with undecided shoppers gravitating online. Retailers who understand this will position a range of in-store and digital offerings to meet consumers where they are."

The most important criteria for back-to-school shoppers remains price. The top two considerations when deciding where to shop are sales and discounts (69%); and competitive prices (57%). While most people also see convenience when shopping, only one-fifth (21%) plan to buy pre-configured school kits from their child's school or Parent Teacher Association/organization.

"Price, product and convenience are the foundation of back-to-school shopping, like reading, writing and arithmetic," added Sides. "Nearly all shoppers are in the market for school supplies, which tend to be most price-driven, and clothing, where children have the greatest influence among all categories in the survey. While big-ticket items have the lowest overall demand, they command the highest average spend."

Mass merchant stores remain dominant, with nearly 90% of respondents planning to visit these stores for back-to-school shopping. Notably, online-only retailers have replaced dollar stores as the No. 2 destination (dollar stores held the second-place ranking for the past two years).

Clothing and accessories account for more than half of back-to-school spending (54%), followed by school supplies (22%), electronic gadgets (13%); and computers and hardware (11%).

More than half (60%) of respondents intend to start their school shopping one month to six weeks before school begins, with late July and early August being the busiest — accounting for $17.3 billion in seasonal spending. Shoppers starting in the two weeks immediately before the start of the school year may spend more in the final rush, with an average spend of $889, or $370 more than the average.

**SOURCE:** Deloitte, 30 Rockefeller Plaza, New York, NY, 10112-0015

## 1 in 3 Say Back-to-School Shopping More Stressful, Expensive Than Holiday Shopping

For millions of parents, back-to-school shopping is dreaded even more than holiday shopping, and about a third of shoppers said it's both more stressful and more expensive, according to a new report from CompareCards by LendingTree.

With the new school year fast approaching, CompareCards asked Americans about back-to-school shopping and found the end-of-summer ritual drives stress, debt and parent-child arguments – and many think their costs will only increase.

Key findings

- 36% think back-to-school shopping is more stressful than holiday shopping, and 32% said it's more expensive.
- 23% said back-to-school shopping has at least somewhat damaged their relationship with their child.
- More than a quarter of shoppers expect to go into debt because of back-to-school shopping, and most will not be able to pay off that debt quickly.
- Half of back-to-school shoppers plan to spend more this year than last year. On average, shoppers expect to spend $428 on back-to-school shopping this year.
- 43% are stressed about how they will pay for back-to-school shopping.

"With parents collectively spending billions of dollars on their children's back-to-school shopping needs each year, it's no wonder the end-of-summer ritual takes a toll on wallets, emotions and even relationships," said Matt Schulz, Chief Industry Analyst at CompareCards. "While it's unlikely shoppers can completely eliminate all stress from the back-to-school season, careful planning and savvy shopping goes a long way. Shoppers can set boundaries and budgets before heading to the mall, use credit card rewards and sign-up bonuses strategically, and comparison shop for the best deals. At the end of the day, back-to-school season happens just once per year, and soon enough the chaos will be over, so breathe, Mom and Dad. You've got this."

**Source:** LendingTree, 11115 Rushmore Drive, Charlotte, NC 28277

# Chapter 20

# Social Media

## Pinterest Leads the Pack in Social Media Customer Satisfaction

Social media users have a low level of satisfaction with the platforms they use as a whole for the second year in a row, this according to a report from the American customer Satisfaction Index (ACSI). The ACSI measures customer satisfaction with 46 industries, and social media currently ranks 6th-lowest following this research, with a score of 72 on a 100-point scale.

A couple of individual social media sites fared somewhat better in customer satisfaction, with Pinterest receiving the highest customer satisfaction score of the tested social platforms again this year. Pinterest's score of 80 remains unchanged from the year before.

Compared with other platforms, Pinterest is relatively small in terms of users, with Pew Research reporting that just more than one-quarter (28%) of U.S. adults use the platform. By comparison, the same report found that YouTube, which has the second-highest customer satisfaction score, is used by nearly three-quarters (73%) of US adults. YouTube's customer satisfaction score of 78 is up 3 points (4%) from 2018.

Dropping 4 points (6%) to a score of 63, Facebook has the lowest customer satisfaction score of all the tested social platforms. The report explains that "the critical measure of privacy is at an all-time low for Facebook — trailing all other social media sites by a wide gap." It also notes that "users also find advertising on Facebook to be more intrusive than other sites."

**Social Media Customer Experience Benchmarks**

Social media users are most satisfied with the mobile aspects of social media. Mobile app quality (80), mobile app reliability (78) and ease of use on different devices such as smartphones and tablets (77) were the top-rated components of social media user experience.

Users also rate site performance (77) and ease of navigation (76) high. However, users are less impressed with factors such as the relevance of content (72), privacy (70) and the amount of ads on sites (68). On these two latter points, a global survey of more than 43,000 consumers by Dentsu Aegis Network showed that many were being proactive with regards to data sharing – 44% had taken actions to limit their data footprint, 1 in 7 had deactivated their social media accounts and more than one-quarter (27%) had installed ad-blocking software in the past 12 months.

**Search Slips Slightly**

Last year, customer satisfaction with search engines rose 3 points. Unable to maintain the 79 point rating into 2019, customer satisfaction fell 2 points to 77 on the 100-point scale. Google's user satisfaction rating dropped 3 points as well to 79, which the report attributes to two data breaches that occurred with its now-defunct Google+ social network.

Much like social media, mobile app quality (84) and reliability of mobile apps (82) were ranked highest in users' experience with search engines. However, other elements saw a decrease in satisfaction, including:

- Ease of navigation (81, down from 83);
- Site performance (80, down from 82);
- Variety of services and information (80, down from 82); and
- Speed and reliability of video clips (79, down from 80).

**Source:** ACSI LLC, 625 Avis Drive, Ann Arbor, MI 48108, (734) 913-0788

# Chapter 21

# TECHNOLOGY

## 1 in Every 10 Adults in the U.S. Doesn't Use the Internet

The amount of U.S. adults who do not use the internet continues its slow decline, according to new data from Pew Research Center, with the percentage of the U.S. adult population who do not use the internet has more than halved in fewer than 10 years. Still, 1 in 10 U.S. adults remain non-internet users.

The new report finds similar patterns of internet usage seen in previous years, with adoption rates strongly correlating with age, household income, educational level, and community type.

It is worth noting that internet usage is consistent among me (90%) and women (90%).

However, despite figures from last year showing consistency among races and ethnicities, this year there is a larger gap in usage between White (92%), Black (85%), Hispanic (86%) adults.

**Age**

Research from AARP has shown that tech usage is regularly increasing among older Americans. However, internet usage remains the lowest among the oldest age group (65+).

Over one-quarter (27%) of adults ages 65 and older do not use the internet, according to the latest study. While this percentage has decreased from nearly one-third (34%) last year, it still means that less than three-quarters (73%) of the 65+ population is active on the internet and can be reached by digital means.

Although marketers are designating more of their digital marketing spending to target Baby Boomers, more traditional forms of marketing and advertising communications are still necessary to catch those adults refraining from online use. Traditional TV might be the best opportunity to reach these individuals since they have been shown to spend more time viewing traditional TV.

Meanwhile, roughly one in eight adults ages 50-64 (12%) do not go online. The percentage drops to 3% of 30-49-year-olds, and Pew's data shows that all 18-29-year-olds they surveyed use the internet.

**Household Income**

Nearly all adults with a household income of at least $50k use the internet, as do the vast majority (93%) of those with a household income of $30-50k. These figures have not changed from 2018.

That said, the number of non-internet users increases substantially among the lowest-income respondents, with 18% of those with a household income under $30K not on the internet.

Despite internet usage increasing over time for this group, it is doing so slowly; in 2013, almost one-quarter (24%) of those household income under $30K were not internet users.

**Educational Level**

Just like with household income, Pew's data sees a correlation between education levels and internet non-usage (i.e., the higher the level of education, the more likely to live a digital life). However, the difference is more noticeable.

Nearly three in 10 (29%) U.S. adults who have less than a high school education do not use the internet. Non-usage falls to 16% for those who obtained a high school diploma, and takes a drastic decline for those with some college (5%) and a college degree (2%).

**Community Type**

Adults who live in urban areas who don't go online increased to 9% this year from 8% last year. However, suburban adults have seen a significant decline in non-internet usage compared to 2018 (6% this year vs. 10% last year).

While a greater number of rural Americans do not use the internet compared to other communities, the number has also decreased in the past year to 15%, from 22%.

**SOURCE:** Pew Research Center, 1615 L Street, NW, Suite 800, Washington, DC 20036

# Chapter 22

# VACATION

## Vacation Savings on the Rise despite Focus on High-End Experiences

CIT Bank's 2019 Summer Savings Survey conducted by The Harris Poll shows that vacations are a rising savings priority for twice as many consumers compared to 2018. The recent survey measures consumer sentiment on topics such as vacation saving and spending trends, financial satisfaction, and overall banking strategies.

"Consumers are taking charge of their finances to make vacations more of a savings priority," said Ravi Kumar, head of Internet Banking for CIT Bank. "We're encouraged by the results of our survey as planning ahead is one of the key habits necessary to improve financial stability and prevent going into debt."

**Gen Z Splurges on High-End Experiences**

Generationally, Gen Z consumers outpace others when it comes to vacation spending across a number of categories, in particular, unique food experiences and luxury hotels. Over 40% of Gen Z consumers like to spend on unique food and drink experiences compared to 34% of Millennials, 35% of Gen X, 26% of Boomers, and 24% of Seniors. Likewise, over a third of Gen Z consumers like to spend on luxury accommodations compared to a quarter of Millennials and Gen Xers and even less Boomers and Seniors. Gen Z also outspends their counterparts on health and relaxation and first or business class transportation accommodations.

**Maximize Vacation Savings with CIT Bank's Savings Builder**

Despite the jump in saving, over a third of consumers are still not saving anything for vacations, suggesting more can be done to prepare for summertime splurges. Another third save less than 5% and approximately a quarter save between 5 to 10% of their monthly income.

CIT Bank's newest digital savings product Savings Builder is designed to reward consistent savers and provides a higher rate for those who make a deposit of at least $100 on a monthly basis.

"Consider stashing away $100 each month to save for vacations ahead of time," continued Kumar. "Doing so can eliminate the financial stress and burden of increased expenditures during the summer when vacation season is at its peak.

**Source:** The Harris Poll

## Americans' Summer Vacation Spending Expected to Hit Record $101.7 Billion in 2019

Americans are planning to spend more on their summer vacations this year than they have in at least a decade. Allianz Global Assistance's 11th annual Vacation Confidence Index estimates the total spend will cross the $100 billion mark for the third consecutive year in the index's history, amounting to $101,700,000,000.

Americans' average anticipated spend on vacations this summer is $2,037, topping $2,000 for the first time since 2010 when the survey started tracking spending, and marking a 5.2% increase over last year. According to the fifth-annual Global Travel Forecast from the Global Business Travel Association and Carlson Family Foundation, travel prices are expected to rise sharply in 2019 due to a growing global economy and rising oil prices.

Nearly half (42%) of Americans believe they will take a vacation this year, nearing its lowest point sine 2013 when only 40% were confident they would take one. More than half of Americans who are not confident (52%) in taking a vacation this summer cited financial reasons, while another four in 10 of those with low confidence (38%) are restricted by time constraints, such as not being able to take time off from work or not wanting to take time off from work.

Just under half (49%) of Americans say they usually take an annual summer vacation, a three percentage point increase from 2018. Most likely to take a vacation are Gen Xers (ages 35-40), high income earners ($100K+) and those who think a vacation is important. Two in 10 Americans (21%) have taken a vacation in the past three months, while more than half of Americans (51%) last took a vacation more than a year ago.

In analyzing travelers' summer vacation spending habits, Allianz found that Americans are predicted to spend over 20% (23.2%) more than they did in 2010 where the average anticipated spend was $1,653.

"Summer vacation spending will hit record levels this year, with Americans planning to spend an average of more than $2,000 on their trip, according to our 11th annual Vacation Confidence Index," said Daniel Durazo, director of marketing and communications at Allianz Global Assistance USA. "This will bring total spending to a record $101 billion, a number which reflects the continued value that Americans place on their summer trips. As the amount spent on vacations continues to increase, it's even more important that consumers purchase travel insurance when they book their trip, in order to protect their travel investment and protect against costly medical emergencies while traveling."

The Vacation Confidence Index has been conducted each summer since 2009 by national polling firm Ipsos Public Affairs on behalf of Allianz Global Assistance USA. A vacation is defined as a leisure trip of at least a week to a place that is 100 miles or more from home.

**SOURCE:** Allianz Global Assistance, P.O. Box 71533, Richmond, VA 23255-1533

# Chapter 23

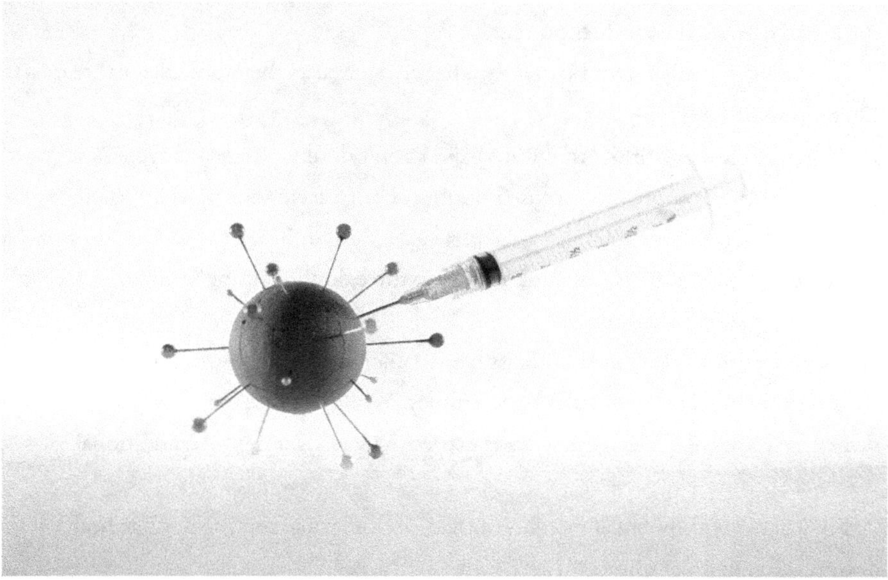

# Vaccines

## 45% of American Adults Doubt Vaccine Safety, According to Survey

An online survey of more than 2,000 U.S. adults recently conducted by The Harris Poll on behalf of the American Osteopathic Association, revealed that more than two in five American adults (45%) say something has caused them to doubt vaccine safety.

The spread of negative attitudes towards vaccines is a phenomenon deeply rooted in human psychology and amplified by social media, according to perinatal psychiatrist Rachel Shmuts, DO.

"From an evolutionary perspective, humans are primed to pay attention to threats or negative information," she says. "So it makes sense that people hold onto fears that vaccines are harmful, especially when they believe their children are in danger."

Because vaccines have been so effective at reducing or eradicating diseases, she believes that some people may have more fear about possible side effects from the vaccines than the actual diseases the vaccines prevent.

"For some, it really might be that vaccines are viewed as the more salient threat," says Dr. Shmuts.

While more than half of Americans (55%) don't doubt vaccine safety, 45% acknowledged at least one source that caused doubts about vaccination safety. Online articles (16%), past secrets/wrongdoing by the pharmaceutical industry (16%) and information from medical experts (12%) are rank as the top three doubt-causing sources.

**No more room for doubt.**

Americans were also asked in the survey to choose a statement that best represented their feelings about vaccine safety and efficacy. While the vast majority (82%) chose in favor of vaccines, 8% selected responses expressing serious doubt. An additional 9% said they were unsure.

Physicians say those small margins can cause significant damage to public health if the doubts result in more unvaccinated people.

"Some diseases, like measles, require as much as 95% of the population to be vaccinated in order to achieve herd immunity," says osteopathic family physician Paul Ehrmann, DO. "Our practice considers itself a steward of public health, so we do not take new patients who refuse to vaccinate."

Dr. Ehrmann explains that herd immunity is essential to maintain, because some people cannot be vaccinated due to medical conditions including allergies, illness, or a weakened immune system. Keeping the rest of the population vaccinated protects those who are vulnerable.

"People know that a lot of practices won't accept patients who don't vaccinate, so when they find one that will, they spread the word to their community that it's a safe place. Whether intentional or not, those doctors are often seen as endorsing anti-vaxxer beliefs," Dr. Ehrmann said.

**Winning patients back**

While social media has helped spread misinformation about vaccines, it has not been effective for countering those claims, even with scientific research, according to Dr. Shmuts.

She explains that confirmation bias—the tendency to trust new information that bolsters existing beliefs and discredit information that challenges those beliefs—makes it difficult to convince someone vaccines are safe, effective and necessary once they believe they are not.

"The number of people who believe vaccines are dangerous and refuse to get them is still relatively small. However, online support groups seem to solidify their beliefs, making them less susceptible to influence from their neighbors and real-world communities," says Dr. Shmuts.

Dr. Ehrmann agrees, adding that arguing or being judgmental with patients only pushes them further into communities that share their beliefs. Instead, he thinks policy changes are likely the most effective means to change behaviors, if not hearts and minds.

His home state of Michigan discontinued public education for vaccines in the mid-2000s and allows for medical, religious and philosophical exemptions for vaccination, making the state accommodating to anti-vaxxers. As recent as 2015, Michigan ranked 44th in the country for the number of vaccinated children 19 months to 35 months.

However, in 2017 the state, with other partners, launched a public information campaign that has significantly improved vaccination rates across demographics.

"Beliefs are hard to change especially when they're based in fear," says Dr. Ehrmann. "But, being responsible for our patients' health and the public's health, we can't afford to give in to those fears. We must insist on evidence-based medicine."

**SOURCE:** American Osteopathic Association, 142 E. Ontario St., Chicago, IL 60611-2864, Phone: (888) 62-MYAOA (888-626-9262)

# Chapter 24

# Weddings

## Forty-Five Percent of Newlyweds Went into Debt for Their Wedding — and It's Causing Marital Problems

Almost half (45%) of newlyweds between the ages of 18 and 53 went into debt to pay for their wedding. And once married, nearly half of the newlyweds who obtained wedding-related debt said money has caused them to consider divorce. On the flip side, only 9% of couples without wedding-related debt contemplate divorce, this according to LendingTree's study on newlyweds and wedding expenses.

Key survey findings:

- 45% of Americans ages 18 to 53 who were married within the last two years went into debt for their wedding.

- 76% of newlyweds who went into debt for their wedding say they argued about wedding-related expenses with their partner. Comparatively, only 20% of those who avoided wedding debt said the same.

- Nearly half (47%) of newlyweds who went into wedding debt say money caused them to contemplate divorce, compared to just 9% of couples who did not go into debt for their wedding.

- 36% of those who had wedding debt say they argue with their partner about money often, versus 11% of couples without wedding debt.

- 1 in 4 newlyweds wish they spent less on their wedding, and their biggest regret was spending too much on food and drink or the venue.

- For about a third of newlyweds (32%), family caused the most headaches during the wedding planning process. Money was the primary stressor for 28%, and 17% reported the guest list as their biggest headache.

**SOURCE:** LendingTree, 11115 Rushmore Drive, Charlotte, NC 28277

# Chapter 25

# Work

## Women Win Promotions Sooner, But Hit Ceiling Sooner, Too

The average number of years for a woman to be promoted to her first manager position is 6.6 years. Men take a bit longer – 7.3 years — for the first step up the corporate ladder.

But each step up the ladder becomes harder for women, the study finds. As women move up management levels, there is a steep decline at the 3rd level of management; this decline becomes more pronounced at each level of advancement.

Managers are paid an average of $47 per hour, while non-managers earn $25.

Women earn $25 an hour, 79% of the $32 for males. The ratio of women pay to men reaches as high as 82% at the fourth level of management, but drops to 77% at the top levels of the firm.

Employees who have managers with more direct reports are more likely to leave the firm.

For example, direct reports' turnover for mangers with 4-6 direct reports is 2.3%; direct reports' turnover for managers with greater than 15 direct reports is 3.5%.

Leisure/Hospitality (11.4 direct reports) and Education/Healthcare (8.5 direct reports) have highest number of direct reports.

Firms are more likely to promote internally to management (17.2%) than make a new hire for management (15.6%)

At the highest level of management, 21.5% are internal promotions while just 12.5% are new hire.

The study is based on payroll data from more than 13 million employees.

Overall, employers promote 8.9% of their employees annually and those employees received an average wage increase of 17.4%.

Interestingly, however, promotions within a team are associated with higher turnover among other team members. Dr. Yildirmaz noted that, "While promotional opportunity may be perceived as a net positive, it can also have negative impact for team members who have been passed over." On the flipside, the probability for promotion exceeds 20 % for employees as they reach higher levels of management within the organization. Firms are more likely to promote internal employees for management positions, and the percentage of internal hires increase for higher levels in the organization.

**SOURCE:** *ADP State of the Workforce Report: Pay, Promotions and Retention*, ADP Research Institute.

## Less Than 1 Million Bicycle to Work

May is National Bike Month, sponsored by the League of American Bicyclists and celebrated in communities from coast to coast. Established in 1956, National Bike Month is a chance to showcase the many benefits of bicycling — and encourage more folks to giving biking a try.

They've got a ways to go. According to the U.S. Census Bureau, about 837,000 workers in the U.S. bicycled to work in 2017 – the latest figures available from the Census Bureau -- down from about 865,000 in 2012 and up from 665,000 in 2007. Of those, 603,577 were male.

Compared to the number of workers driving to work – 130,340,856 – the number of bicyclists is a minuscule number.

**SOURCE:** Table B08006, Sex of Workers by Means of Transportation to Work, Universe: Workers 16 years and over, American Community Survey, 1 year estimates, U.S. Census Bureau.

## More Than Half of U.S. Employees Who Typically Eat Lunch During Work Hours Struggle to Make It Healthy

When it comes to employed Americans, more than half (56%) who typically eat lunch during work hours struggle to make it healthy, and more than three-quarters (77%) say they're more likely to make healthier decisions at other times of the day if they eat healthy at lunch. This according to a new survey from the American Heart Association, the leading voluntary health organization devoted to a world of longer, healthier lives, and Aramark, the largest U.S. based food service company.

The survey was conducted online by The Harris Poll on behalf of the American Heart Association and Aramark as part of their joint initiative, Healthy for Life 20 By 20, among 907 employed U.S. adults aged 18 or older who say they typically eat lunch during work hours.

"Understanding what employees are eating for lunch on a typical workday and what factors influence their choices helps us develop strategies to improve dietary intake with multi-level approaches through food systems, communities and individuals," said Anne Thorndike, MD, MPH, vice chair of the American Heart Association's Nutrition Committee and associate professor at Harvard Medical School. "The finding that healthier food choices at work may impact food choices throughout the rest of the day presents a unique opportunity for the workplace to have a positive influence on not only the employee's health but also the health of the employee's family."

The survey of employed U.S. adults who typically eat lunch during work hours found that:

- **More than 9 in 10** (91%) **are interested in improving the healthfulness of their typical workday lunch** with employees under 40 more likely to be extremely/very interested compared to employees aged 40+ (65% vs. 55%).

- **More than 4 in 5** (82%) **agree that having healthy food options at work is important** to them and more than 2 in 3 (68%) value help from their employer in becoming healthier.

- **About 4 in 5** (79%) whose workplace has on-site cafeteria, food service or vending machines get food there at least some of the time.

- **Nearly 9 in 10** (86%) **prepare work lunches at home at least some of the time**, with women more likely to do so than men (91% vs. 82%).

- **When eating an unhealthy lunch, employees under age 40 are more likely to be impacted at least a little bit by cost** (91% vs. 79%) **and choices of their peers or coworkers** (75% vs. 50%) than employees aged 40+.

- **On a stressful day at work, about 1 in 3** (35%) **say their lunch is less healthy than a typical day**, with women more likely to say so than men (40% vs 32%).

Motivated by its mission to enrich and nourish lives and its Healthy for Life 20 By 20 collaboration with the American Heart Association to improve the health of all Americans, Aramark launched a major plant-forward initiative to boost nutrition across its menus in colleges and universities, hospital cafés and workplace locations. The initiative has resulted in a 15% average reduction in calories, saturated fat and sodium, and significant increases in fruits, vegetables and whole grains across those dining location menus.

"Aramark and the American Heart Association are proud of our shared commitment to help millions of people lead healthier lives," says Dan Wainfan, vice president, Brand Health, Wellness and Nutrition at Aramark. "Through this survey, and as part of extensive consumer insights gained throughout our Healthy for Life 20 By 20 initiative, consumers are emphasizing that health and wellness is top of mind every day. While they don't always make a healthy choice, they always want delicious, healthy choices available—at work and at home."

While employees who typically eat lunch during work hour cite limited availability of healthy foods (43%) as having a great deal/quite a bit of impact on eating an unhealthy lunch, more of these employees cite convenience (60%) and taste preference (54%) as having a great deal/quite a bit of impact on choosing an unhealthy lunch.

"Improving the nutrition content and reducing calories of classic favorites and typically indulgent menu items helps. Having more plant-based options to choose from at home and on menus helps. But in the end, people still need to choose to eat healthier food. The good news is most people said they are interested in doing better," said Thorndike.

**Source:** The Harris Poll, 155 Corporate Woods, Rochester, NY 14623, (585) 272-8400

## Half of Employed Adults Likely to Job Hunt Next Year

Almost half of adults in the U.S. (48%) who are currently employed are likely to look for a new job in the next year, this according to the results of the latest American Staffing Association Workforce Monitor survey conducted online by The Harris Poll.

This includes transitioning to an entirely new career, not just finding a new job. Four in 10 adults currently working (38%) say they are likely to change careers (e.g., switch to a new industry or field, or a different position or role) within the next year, as do one in two Millennials (51%) and one in three members of Gen X (34%).

Many do not believe that landing their ideal job is a future possibility, as four in 10 working adults (44%) are worried they will never find the perfect job for them. Opinions differ based on employee occupation. Notably, half of those working in the office–administrative (51%), industrial (48%), and professional–managerial (47%) industry sectors lack confidence that they will ever find their ideal job, while one in four in health care (39%) and one in three in the engineering, IT, and scientific sector (32%) share this concern. And seven in 10 students (69%) also worry about finding the right job.

"The U.S. is immersed in the tightest labor market in modern history with millions of unfilled openings across geographies and industries," said Richard Wahlquist, ASA president and chief executive officer. "It's a job seeker's market—a reality lost on many people who, as the ASA Workforce Monitor shows, sadly lack optimism about their prospects of finding a perfect position."

**Source:** The Harris Poll, 155 Corporate Woods, Rochester, NY 14623, (585) 272-8400

# Chapter 26

# PHOTO SOURCES

Gaming: Photo by Kaysha on Unsplash

Guns: Morristown Mass Shooting ProtestCredit: Tom W. Sulcer (CC0)

Housing: Photo by Blake Wheeler on Unsplash

Internet: Photo by Jadon Kelly on Unsplash

Jobs: Photo by Clem Onojeghuo on Unsplash

Marriage: Photo by Sandy Millar on Unsplash

Medical: Photo by Julia Zyablova on Unsplash

Millennials: Photo by Eileen Pan on Unsplash

Politics: Photo by Clay Banks on Unsplash

Retailers: Photo by Heidi Fin on Unsplash

School: Photo by Element5 Digital on Unsplash

Social Media: Photo by Adem AY on Unsplash

Technology: Photo by Marvin Meyer on Unsplash

Vacation: Photo by Vicko Mozara on Unsplash

Vaccines: Photo by Iván Díaz on Unsplash

Weddings: Photo by Sooz . on Unsplash

Work: Photo by Merakist on Unsplash

www.ingramcontent.com/pod-product-compliance
Lightning Source LLC
LaVergne TN
LVHW022010200926
848481LV00007B/2314
*9780940195035*